Womanist Ethical Rhetoric

Rhetoric, Race, and Religion

Series Editor: Andre E. Johnson, University of Memphis

This series will provide space for emerging, junior, or senior scholars engaged in research that studies rhetoric from a race or religion perspective. This will include studies contributing to our understanding of how rhetoric helps shape race and/or religion and how race and/or religion shapes rhetoric. In this series, scholars seek to examine phenomenon from either a historical or contemporary perspective. Moreover, we are interested in how race and religion discourse function rhetorically.

Recent Titles in This Series

Rhetorics of Race and Religion on the Christian Right: Barack Obama and the War on Terror
By Samuel P. Perry
Rhetoric, Race, Religion, and the Charleston Shootings: Was Blind But Now I See
By Sean Patrick O'Rourke and Melody Lehn
Rhetoric and the Responsibility to and for Language: Speaking of Evil
By Matthew Boedy
The Struggle over Black Lives Matter and All Lives Matter
By Amanda Nell Edgar and Andre E. Johnson
Desegregation and the Rhetorical Fight for African American Citizenship Rights
By Sally F. Paulson
Contemporary Christian Culture: Messages, Missions, and Dilemmas
Edited by Omotayo Banjo Adesagba and Kesha Morant Williams
The Motif of Hope in African American Preaching during Slavery and the Post-Civil War Era: There's a Bright Side Somewhere
By Wayne E. Croft
The Womanist Preacher: Proclaiming Womanist Rhetoric from the Pulpit
By Kimberly P. Johnson
Women Bishops and Rhetorics of Shalom: A Whole Peace
By Leland G. Spencer
What Movies Teach about Race: Exceptionalism, Erasure, and Entitlement
By Roslyn M. Satchel
Womanist Ethical Rhetoric: A Call for Liberation and Social Justice in Turbulent Times
Edited by Annette D. Madlock and Cerise L. Glenn

Womanist Ethical Rhetoric

A Call for Liberation and Social Justice in Turbulent Times

Edited by
Annette D. Madlock
and Cerise L. Glenn

LEXINGTON BOOKS
Lanham • Boulder • New York • London

Published by Lexington Books
An imprint of The Rowman & Littlefield Publishing Group, Inc.
4501 Forbes Boulevard, Suite 200, Lanham, Maryland 20706
www.rowman.com

6 Tinworth Street, London SE11 5AL, United Kingdom

British Library Cataloguing in Publication Information Available

Library of Congress Cataloging-in-Publication Data

Names: Madlock, Annette D., editor. | Glenn, Cerise L., 1977–, editor.
Title: Womanist ethical rhetoric : a call for liberation and social justice in turbulent
    times / edited by Annette D. Madlock and Cerise L. Glenn.
Description: Lanham : Lexington Books, [2020] | Series: Rhetoric, race, and religion |
    Includes bibliographical references and index. | Summary: "Womanist thought
    remains of critical importance given contemporary issues of social justice and
    advocacy. Womanist Ethical Rhetoric centers discourses of religious rhetoric and
    its influence on Black women's aims for voice, empowerment, and agency in these
    turbulent times"—Provided by publisher.
Identifiers: LCCN 2020041917 (print) | LCCN 2020041918 (ebook) |
    ISBN 9781793613554 (cloth) | ISBN 9781793613578 (pbk)
    ISBN 9781793613561 (ebook)
Subjects: LCSH: Womanism. | Womanist theology. | Social justice. | Women,
    Black—Social conditions.
Classification: LCC HQ1197 .W659 2020 (print) | LCC HQ1197 (ebook) |
    DDC 305.48/896073—dc23
LC record available at https://lccn.loc.gov/2020041917
LC ebook record available at https://lccn.loc.gov/2020041918

In honor of the Rev. Dr. Katie Geneva Cannon (1950–2018)
Katie Geneva Cannon was the first African American woman ordained in the United Presbyterian Church (USA), and her work focused on the areas of Christian ethics, Womanist theology, and women in religion and society. She lectured nationally on theological and ethical topics. She was the author or editor of numerous articles and seven books, including Katie's Canon: Womanism and the Soul of the Black Community and Black Womanist Ethics.

ℰↃ

Cerise dedicates this book to her mother, Jo Linda Parham Glenn (1952–2018). Your legacy continues to live on in the work of the lives you have touched. We love and miss you. Annette dedicates this book to the following women as their work and dedication to their families and communities speaks to our lived experiences and exemplifies a womanist ethic of liberation and Black feminist thought: Dr. Melbourne S. Cummings, Carla Bradford, Rev. Dr. Alika P. Galloway, Gwen Ifill, Carolyn Madlock, Danna Madlock, and Dr. Denise Dunbar-Perkins.

Contents

Acknowledgments ix

Introduction: A Womanist Canon: Honoring the Legacy of
Black Women xiii
Cerise L. Glenn and Annette D. Madlock

1 Voicing a Womanist Ethic of Liberation and Social Justice
among the Religious Right 1
Annette D. Madlock

2 A Womanist Response to Black Lives Matter and American
Nationalism 17
Kimberly P. Johnson

3 Examining Grace Greenleaf: Black Women's Activism
and Spirituality 33
Cerise L. Glenn

4 "The Beloved Language Community": A Call for
Womanism and Language to Address the Racial Academic
Achievement Gap 51
Kami J. Anderson

5 Is There Room for the Ratchet in the Beloved Community?:
If You're Not Liberating Everyone, Are You Really Talking
about Freedom? 63
Michelle Meggs

6 "Women, Step Forward!": Doing Rhetorical Historiography
    by Exploring Womanist Leadership in the AME Church   77
    Natonya Listach and Andre E. Johnson

7 "I Am My Sisters' Keeper": Invitational Rhetoric and
    Womanist Theology   91
    Tracy Coquette Bass and Michelle Rhnea Yisrael

Conclusion   103
Annette D. Madlock and Cerise L. Glenn

Index   105

About the Editors   109

About the Contributors   111

Acknowledgments

Some of us have people in our lives with whom we share and discuss our ideas; Dr. Andre E. Johnson is one of those people for me. As I shared my ideas about social justice, womanist rhetoric, and Black feminist thought, Dr. Johnson extended to me the opportunity to be a part of the Rhetoric Race and Religion series (R3). Thank you, Andre, for listening and supporting me along the way as you have done for so many others. After further contemplation, I decided on an edited collection to include the voices of other scholar-activists. I invited Dr. Cerise L. Glenn to work with me on the collection as a coeditor. We both come to the project committed to social activism, womanism, and black feminist perspectives. When you have an idea for a project, it takes a community to make it all come together, and this is an opportunity for me to thank those who contributed to making this project happen.

That community includes the scholars who participated in the following panel: *Womanist Rhetorical Theory and Criticism* for the African American Rhetoric and Public Address (AARPA) Pre-Conference at the 2019 National Communication Association conference: Ayo Morton, Kimberly P. Johnson, Tiffany J. Bell, Dianna Watkins-Dickerson, and Toniesha L. Taylor. We had an excellent exchange of ideas regarding the application of womanist and black feminist thought from diverse perspectives to various contexts.

Communicating for survival was the theme for both the 2019 National Communication Association convention and the Religious Communication Association conference, which allowed me to continue on the womanist path by organizing, presenting, and responding to the following conference panels: *Communication for survival: Where's the beloved community?*, *Social justice, religion, and the 21st-century church*, and a *Womanist ethic of liberation and social justice in the current political climate from academics to organizational leadership*. Thank you, Kami J. Anderson, Christopher House,

Christopher Underation, and the panelists from the AARPA preconference. The exchange of ideas during these well-attended panels created additional opportunities for sharing womanist scholarship.

Coordinating the conference panels created an opportunity for me to continue facilitating the exchange of ideas by serving as guest editor for the special issue "A Womanist Rhetorical Vision for Building the Beloved Community" for the *Journal of Communication and Religion.* Serving as guest editor was another opportunity to make space for womanist scholarship centered on issues of social justice and equity from a variety of sociocultural circumstances. Not every panelist appears in the journal special issue or this edited collection, but their participation is part of the collective work for the larger project. All of our work is part of the zeitgeist as we strive for the common goal of social equity.

With much humility, I thank you.

Annette D. Madlock

Thank you to my partner and husband, Robert L. Manigault, Jr., and my brother, Willis L. Glenn, III. You continue to be my strongest support system, and I love and appreciate both of you. Rob, I am especially grateful for your support, care, patience, and being a sounding board during my writing sessions. Willis, dear brother and confidant, I always appreciate your mix of advocacy and criticism to challenge me to push forward with my ideas. It is important to have people in my corner who know the strengths and potential pitfalls of my work. Both of your support and critique with love always help me to continually grow as a person and scholar.

My academic path has been one that's more circuitous than a straight line. I am grateful to have the continual support of one of my first professors, Dr. Dee James, whom I met when I was seventeen years old. Dee, I am fortunate to have you as a mentor. Your work supervising me as a tutor in the university Writing Center and advising my first primary research project when I was an undergraduate continues to help me channel my voice into writing and research. I still use the many lessons you taught me and an appreciative of your mentoring and support throughout my career in academia.

I would also like to acknowledge my Howard University family for being the best mix of support and encouragement with challenging questions to keep me work to strengthen my academic skills. Dr. Melbourne Cummings, Dr. William Starosta, and Dr. Ahbik Roy, especially, helped me develop my line of inquiry into Black feminist thought and womanist perspectives. I appreciate the extra time in the office and during summers to help me push through challenging experiences and encouraging me to stay true to my path.

I would finally like to acknowledge my dear friend and colleague Dr. Annette D. Madlock. When we met as graduate students, I was excited to have academic and personal conversations about contemporary issues and scholarship. Our conversations about Black feminism and womanism have helped me grow over the years and during the course of working on this edited collection. I especially appreciate being able to work with you on this important book in the Rhetoric Race and Religion series (R3), edited by Dr. Andre Johnson. I am honored to be part of this homage to my mother and womanist scholars/activists who continue to advocate for social justice.

Cerise L. Glenn

Introduction

A Womanist Canon: Honoring the Legacy of Black Women

Cerise L. Glenn and Annette D. Madlock

Rev. Dr. Katie Cannon opens the third chapter of her seminal book on womanist theology, *Katie's Canon: Womanism and the Soul of the Black Community*, with this quote:

> The feminist consciousness of Afro-American women cannot be understood and explained adequately apart from the historical context in which Black women have found themselves as moral agents. By tracking down the central and forma-tive facts in the Black woman's social world, one can identify the determinant and determining structures of oppression that have shaped the context in which Black women discriminately and critically interpret Scripture, in order to appre-hend the divine Word from the perspective of their own situation. Throughout the history of the United States, the interrelationship of White supremacy and male superiority has characterized the Black woman's reality as a situation of struggle—a struggle to survive in two contradictory worlds simultaneously, one White, privileged, and oppressive, the other Black, exploited, and oppressed. Thus, an untangling of the Black religious heritage sheds light on the feminist consciousness that guides Black women in their ongoing struggle for survival.[1]

This chapter, aptly titled "The Emergence of a Black Feminist Consciousness," serves as a call for empowering the voices and lives of Black women who have been largely omitted from religious discourses. In this edited collection, my coeditor, Dr. Annette D. Madlock, and I pay homage to Katie Cannon's work as we continue the work of her legacy in socially turbulent times affecting African American communities. Cannon, the first African American woman ordained in the United Presbyterian Church, focused her work on womanism, Black feminism, and ethics in theology. As such, we honor her and other

Black women who have come before us through examining the long-storied marginalization we encounter in religious and other social spaces. In doing this work, we center African American women's rhetorical positioning. We do that in a discipline that still largely centers Western thought and privileges masculine voices. Our lives are entrenched in remnants of past and contemporary iterations of multiple forms of marginalization, including racism and sexism. Katie Cannon's life and seminal work greatly influenced and centered the lived experiences of Black women in religion. By disputing notions of white supremacy and patriarchy in her work, she calls for recognizing the voices of Black women, who have largely been omitted and marginalized. She centers intersectional voices in womanist thought, calling for inclusion of all Black women and not just those who aspire to reach/achieve the politics of respectability projected upon them by others.

Our collection of chapters centers womanist approaches to liberation and social justice in turbulent times. As we, as editors and contributors, address this call, we continue to strive and make advancements in a variety of areas. We continue to navigate the complicated tension—one of marginalization and empowerment. This tension becomes reproduced and replicated in multiple ways as African Americans, a culturally communal group, work together. One such mechanism is religion, often referred to as the Black church, in many African American communities—which becomes more nuanced in contemporary times as African Americans become more class and geographically stratified.[2] Yet it remains an important and vital aspect of advocacy and social justice. Like other institutions, the meaning and significance change over time. As we examine these changes, we stand on the shoulders of our womanist predecessors and pay homage to them, most notably Rev. Dr. Katie Cannon, as we advance the legacy of her work on womanism and religion.

CHANGING THE CANON-KATIE CANNON'S LEGACY

Katie Cannon's seminal book on womanist theology centers Black women's spiritual identities. By doing so, she addresses ways our contributions have been omitted, silenced, and overtly oppressed in multiple institutions, including religious doctrine and spaces. As the title of her seminal book, *Katie's Canon: Womanism and the Soul of the Black Community*, connotes, Black women must strive to change the canon as we remain marginalized by dominant frames of thought.[3] Popular definitions of the word *canon* entail "a general law, rule, principle, or criterion by which something is judged" and "a collection or list of sacred books accepted as genuine" or "the works of a particular author or artist that are recognized as genuine."[4] As such, with her last name of *Cannon*, she makes the rhetorical move of writing herself into the knowledge system in religious communities. She transforms the religious rhetoric of Black womanhood with the simplicity of acknowledging we exist. As simple as this sounds, it becomes complex to challenge the "traditional" rhetorical framing of Black womanhood, which has been largely ignored through omission, and even when we are acknowledged, it is often done so in very limiting, marginalizing ways. Jennings notes that Cannon works toward giving Black women voice and humanizing our experiences as she "refutes the Christian ethical amorality and immorality of blacks and identifies the writings of black women as repositories for understanding the ethical values and moral wisdom of the black community" (p. 348).[5]

Cannon's lived experiences, in addition to her published works, speak to the ways in which Black women continue to strive for voice, recognition, and inclusion in organized religious spaces. Katie Cannon, born on January 3, 1950, was a native of North Carolina. She spent her childhood in segregated Kannapolis, North Carolina, north of Charlotte, North Carolina. Today, Kannapolis is considered by many to be a suburb of Charlotte, North Carolina's largest metropolitan city, due to recent development and growth in the area; however, during Cannon's childhood, it was quite a different living experience. It was a more rural area where the "Klu Klux Klan still rise at their whim and will." In addition to segregation and other forms of blatant racism, she navigated gender oppression and thus experienced how the two intersected. There were very limited options for Black women: work as a domestic, do hard labor at a mill, or be part of a small, elite group of women who could do the "dignified life-giving work of teaching" in grade school.[6] As I write from my residence near Kannapolis, North Carolina, and reflect upon my upbringing and the women of my family in the Southeast, her story is the story of many Black women of her generation and those who preceded her. My mother, Jo Linda Parham Glenn, to whom this book is also dedicated, has told me stories of working in the mill in South Carolina and contemplating her future.

Not content with any of these limited options and a desire to leave the trauma of racial terrorism, gendered oppression, and perils of poverty, Katie Cannon left North Carolina to pursue her education. Later, she pursued degrees in divinity and returned to her home state. Throughout her pathway to bring womanism to the realm of theology, she earned multiple degrees from various institutions, including a bachelor of Science (Barber-Scotia College), a master of Divinity (Johnson C. Smith Theological Seminary), and a master's and doctoral degree in Philosophy (Union Theological Seminary). As previously noted, Cannon became the first African American woman to be ordained in the United Presbyterian Church in 1974 in Shelby, North Carolina. Cannon also had a career as a professor, including an associate professor of religion at Temple University. She worked to establish the Center for Womanist Leadership at Union Presbyterian Seminary and Society for the Study of Black Religion, in addition to her scholarship in womanism and feminism in religious studies. She won numerous awards throughout her education career and ministry, including the Excellence in Theological Education Award. Katie Cannon's accolades and trailblazing career continue to influence religious rhetoric and womanist thought, as well as everyday experiences of Black women. Even after her passing in 2018, she continues to motivate and inspire Black women and members of other communities. Her legacy continues through the work of Black women, including my mother, who also passed in 2018 and was pursuing becoming an ordained minister when she was called home. She and many other African American women utilized education as a means to different career and personal paths, while also contributing to their religious and spiritual communities. These women, past and present, negotiate our career and spiritual paths and the racial and gendered contradictions we continue to experience. Through this collection, we hope to honor their lives and build upon their experiences.

WOMANIST APPROACHES TO LIBERATION AND SOCIAL JUSTICE IN TURBULENT TIMES

We celebrate how Black women encourage and uplift ourselves in holistic ways that center love and community from womanist perspectives in this collection. As we do, we also acknowledge the tensions and struggles that occur when we continue to be marginalized in various spaces. As noted in the opening quote, Katie Cannon describes womanism as "an untangling of the Black religious heritage sheds light on the feminist consciousness that guides Black women in their ongoing struggle for survival."[7] In light of recent social injustices regarding the deaths of George Floyd, Ahmaud Arbery, Breonna Taylor, among others, by the hands of the police and those claiming social power to police Black lives, it is even more evident that we need to continue to strive for Civil Rights in African American communities. Black Lives Matter. However, with gender dynamics, Black women's stories and voices do not always center Black women—in the form of being recognized both as activist leaders and as recipients of heinous acts of systemic oppression. Our roles are sometimes defined as raising and uplifting Black males, with less attention being paid to our injustices. It's not often publicized that Black Lives Matter was founded by three Black women. The calls for justice for Breonna Taylor have moved slower and received less attention than for George Floyd. We have seen Black women post on social media calls to protect their sons with no mention of their own personal safety. This is not a new issue. Black women have a long-standing history of working to have our voices heard by dominant voices, both within and external to Black communities. We have made progress. Breonna Taylor's case has seen recent momentum, garnered in part by publicity from professional athletes in the National Basketball Association and the Women's National Basketball Association. Joe Biden, the Democratic presidential nominee, is considering prominent Black female politicians to be his running mate as vice president.

As communication scholars, we center discourses—in this instance various notions of religious rhetoric and their influence on Black women's aims for voice, empowerment, and social justice in these turbulent times. The chapters use womanism, in conjunction with other frames, to examine how Black women incorporate different aspects of our identities into our struggles for empowerment and celebrations of who we are in holistic ways that center love and community. Our edited collection begins by examining Black women's spiritual and professional identities among those identifying with belief systems of the religious right, often associated with conservative values centering white masculine notions of Christianity. We then move to a national landscape that analyzes the role of Black churches in Black Lives Matter, reflecting tensions and advancements of activism through more formal organizations and with protests on the ground. The third chapter continues to explore the macro landscape of Black womanhood in religious spaces in popular culture, particularly through leadership and activism, using tenets of womanism and Black feminist thought. The next two chapters expand the notion of a beloved community to address racial academic achievement gaps and inclusion of all Black women, specifically those who do not adhere to norms of "good" Christian Black womanhood. The sixth chapter explores womanist leadership in the AME church, contributing a historical perspective to contemporary issues. Finally, the collection concludes with an invitational rhetorical approach to Black women helping each other through sisterhood. Our collection embraces both the commonalities and differences between womanists through both theoretical and applied contexts. Embracing both allows us to centralize the plurality of Black women's lives, which is key to advancing our voices.

NOTES

1. Katie Cannon, *Katie's Canon: Womanism and the Soul of the Black Community* (New York, NY: Continuum, 1995), 47.

2. Ronald L. Jackson II, Amber L. Johnson, Michael L. Hecht, and Sidney A. Ribeau, *African American Communication: Examining the Complexities of Lived Experiences* (New York: Routledge, 2020).

3. Cannon, *Katie's Canon*, 47.

4. "Canon Definition," Google, accessed June 22, 2020, https://www.google.com
/search?ei=UeHwXofPNLCl_QaZx5jgAQ&q=canon+definition&oq=canon+de&gs_
lcp=CgZwc3ktYWIQARgAMgoIABCxAxBGEPkBMgIIADICCAAyAggAMgI
IADICCAAyAggAMgIIADICCAAyAggAOgQIABBHOgcIABCxAxBDOgQIAB
BDOgUIABCxA1CoBViKFWCeHWgAcAF4AIABkwOIAdMHkgEHMi0xLjEuM
ZgBAKABAoBB2d3cy13aXo&sclient=psy-ab.
5. La Vinia D. Jennings, "Katie's Canon: Womanism and the Soul of the Black
Community," review of *Katie's Canon,* by Katie Cannon, *African American
Review*, 1998.
6. Sara Lawrence-Lightfoot, foreword to *Katie's Canon: Womanism and the Soul
of the Black Community*, by Katie Cannon (United Kingdom: Continuum, 1995).
7. Cannon, *Katie's Canon*, 47.

BIBLIOGRAPHY

Cannon, Katie G. 1995. *Katie's Canon: Womanism and the Soul of the Black
Community. Community*. New York, NY: Continuum.
Google. n.d. " Canon Definition." Accessed June 22, 2020. https://www.google
.com/search?ei=UeHwXofPNLCl_QaZx5jgAQ&q=canon+definition&oq=canon
+de&gs_lcp=CgZwc3ktYWIQARgAMgoIABCxAxBGEPkBMgIIADICCAAyAg
gAMgIIADICCAAyAggAMgIIADICCAAyAggAOgQIABBHOgcIABCx
AxBDOgQIABBDOgUIABCxA1CoBViKFWCeHWgAcAF4AIABkwOIAd
MHkgEHMi0xLjEuMZgBAKABAoBB2d3cy13aXo&sclient=psy-ab.
Jackson II, Ronald L., Johnson, Amber L., Hecht, Michael L., and Sidney A. Ribeau.
(2020). *African American Communication: Examining the Complexities of Lived
Experiences*. New York: Routledge.
Jennings, La Vinia D. 1998. "Katie's Canon: Womanism and the Soul of the Black
Community." Review of *Katie's Canon: Womanism and the Soul of the Black
Community*, by Katie Canon. *African American Review*, 1998.
Lawrence-Lightfoot, Sara. Foreword to *Katie's Canon: Womanism and the Soul of
the Black Community*, by Katie Canon. New York, NY: Continuum, 1995.

Chapter 1

Voicing a Womanist Ethic of Liberation and Social Justice among the Religious Right

Annette D. Madlock

The death of George Floyd and the COVID-19 pandemic have brought the social inequalities that ravage the Black community and other communities of color in the United States to national and global attention. Communities of women and men, young and old, have taken to the streets in protest. In the words of our foremother, Josepine St. Pierre Ruffin (The Women's Era):

> for the sake of our own dignity, the dignity of our race, and the future good name of our children, it is "mete, right, and our bounded duty" to stand forth and declare ourselves and our principles, to teach an ignorant and suspicious world that our aims and interests are identical with those of all good aspiring women. Too long have we been silent under unjust and unholy charge; we cannot expect to have them removed until we disprove them through ourselves.[1]

These are words that represent the sentiments of many and why one must have a voice in these turbulent times.

In the current political climate, sharply divided along the lines of race, religion, and socioeconomics, there is the danger of a single story[2] regarding conservative Evangelical Christians most often equated as the religious right. This is a single story perpetuated by the media (liberal, progressive, conservative)[3] that shapes and frames a picture of Evangelical Christians[4] equated to Make America Great Again (MAGA) Trump supporters. This rhetorical frame is an agenda set by the media that neglects the stories of those Evangelicals who might hold more progressive, moderate, or liberal views. There is no denying the existence of a select group of individuals within this conservative Evangelical Christian demographic that long for the days of the not-so-distant past (where slave codes and black codes prevailed).

Historically this is a past filled with bigotry and hatred toward Black people and other people of color in the United States.

At the same time, there are the conservative right-winged media outlets that report alternative facts, declare opposing factual news stories as fake, and state that systemic racism is a myth that does not exist in this country. This tactic, to some, is suggestive evidence that civil rights, issues of social justice and equality, and #Black Lives Matter are not on the list of conservative white Evangelical Christian priorities. Priorities that center on advocating pro-life, dismantling affordable health care, opposing the human rights of poor people, immigrants, and the LGBTQIAP (Lesbian, Gay, Bisexual, Transgender, Queer, Intersex, Asexual, and Pansexual) community, to name just a few of their political priorities. However, there is a strategy for this agenda that some call the "Conservative Playbook."[5] For all sides involved, liberal and conservative alike, there is a set agenda put forth by each to tell a single story; however, one needs to remember that there is always more to the story. The danger of these stories is that it places Black people as invisible, a muted group, voiceless, or with select voices at best (those voices that represent or support a particular agenda). This chapter looks at the challenges of voicing a womanist ethic of liberation and social justice within these single stories (conservative, liberal, moderate, or progressive). A womanist ethic that demands that we manage and control the narrative of our community that speaks truth to political power.

THE WOMANIST ETHIC OF LIBERATION

"Womanism" is a term that has an often-quoted etymology, which will be summarized here. Walker first used womanism in her 1979 short story "Coming Apart," published in Laura Lederer's anthology *Take Back the Night*.[6] In 1983, Alice Walker shared with the world a four-part definition in her text *In Search of Our Mother's Gardens*. In summary, the first part of the description emphasizes the importance of women handing down their wisdom from one generation of women to the next. Second, it highlights the importance of communal thought and action. Third, the definition critiques the Eurocentric standard of beauty imposed upon Black women. Fourth, womanism itself is used as a counter to the limitations of White feminist thought and activism as it is ineffective in dealing with issues of race and class. When discussing the etymology of the term "womanism" and the womanist idea, one must also remember to include the work of Chikwenye Okonojo Ogunyemi (African Womanism) and Clenora Hudson-Weems (Africana Womanism).[7] Walker, Ogunyemi, and Hudson-Weems each worked to "form the collective basis for an interpolated field of theory and praxis used by a host of people to follow."[8]

The womanist tradition captured my attention because of my vocation as a higher education professional. Womanism has an emphasis on communal thought and antioppression (anti all of the "isms" that bind and foster inequality) activism. Phillips provides explanations for womanism in this way:

> Womanism is a social change perspective rooted in Black Women's and other women of color's everyday experiences and everyday methods of problem solving in everyday spaces, extended to the problem of ending all forms of oppression for all people, restoring the balance between people and the environment/ nature, and reconciling human life with the spiritual dimension.[9]

I answered a call to missions and accepted an assignment in an educational environment that is theopolitical and hostile to those with opposing (religious and political) views, an organization with a contrived presence on conservative media outlets. As I discussed in an issue of *Listening/Journal of Communication, Ethics, Religion, and Culture*,[10] listening for God's call includes work outside of the church in one's chosen profession. There is a concept called the Theology of Work,[11] which helped to clarify my decision to listen to God's voice and take a new journey.[12] Janet Woodlock (2018),[13] in her article "Vocational Discernment and Female Experience of Pastoral Ministry Call," states, "Individual discernment of God-given vocations occurs in a social context." The context for this call is a White Christian Evangelical institution of higher education with a fundamentalist segregationist history. A treacherous journey for a Black woman with womanist liberationist tendencies (antioppressionist).

Womanist and Black feminist theories are culturally based perspectives that take into consideration the contextual and interactive effects of history, culture, race, class, gender, and other forms of oppression and fragmentation.[14] These frameworks provide a contextualized understanding of African American women's life spanning experiences and perspectives. Perspectives that culminate in emancipation and freedom for women. They are collectively a continuation of intellectual and activist traditions that continue to develop over time and push for equality and liberation. Womanism specifically leaves space for solutions that work for the good of the whole community rather than merely the interest of women. A womanist ethic centers on the ethical and moral choices that Black women make as foundational discourse.[15]

Katie G. Cannon discusses how Black women are often compelled to act or to refrain from action under the powers and principalities of the external world; Black womanists search the scriptures to learn how to dispel the threats and fight for the oppressed. The Black womanist identifies with those biblical characters who hold on to life in the face of formidable oppression. The Black womanist tradition motivates one to chip away at oppressive structures. It identifies those texts that help Black womanists to celebrate and rename the numerous incidents of unpredictability in empowering ways.[16] The Black womanist tradition is used as a frame, as this chapter explores how one might communicate a womanist ethic of liberation and social justice among the religious right in a divisive political climate—in essence, countering the single story in a contested space to assist in controlling the narrative about Black people and other oppressed groups.

MEDIA NARRATIVES

The black press was and continues to be extremely important to the community where I grew up.

> For a time, the narrative of the black press and Black America were intertwined because there were no other outlets covering the African-American experience—only the black press carried the news, expressed the pain and outrage and joy and triumph of the black community.[17]

As I reflect, individuals and families took the time to read the various local newspapers (*Milwaukee Courier*,[18] *Milwaukee Community Journal*,[19] *Milwaukee Journal*), watch the local news, and listen to the news on local black radio. Staying current with the community and national news was just what people did. Even with the shrinking pages or the disappearance of printed papers, many continue to get their information this way. For instance, my mom continues to get some of her news from the local print media. For her national news, Lester Holt is the gospel; she has her DVR set for him, and members of her peer group still discuss how Shirley Chisolm should have been president (when your mom puts her friends on speakerphone to talk politics). But the internet and social media have changed the way traditional media outlets deliver information and how news is consumed; even my mom uses her smartphone to stay current with news and events. It is essential to take note of this everyday experience with the media for this generation[20] and others.

One Pew Research article identifies seven areas regarding Black Americans perceptions of the media,

1. A third of Black adults trust information from local news organizations.
2. Black adults are more likely to feel connected to their main source of news.
3. Black adults are more likely to say news organizations keep an eye on political leaders, deal fairly with all sides.

4. Black Americans are less concerned about made-up/fake news than other national issues. (They are more concerned about social issues such as drug addiction, racism, violent crime, the gap between rich and poor, affordable health care, U.S. political system, and climate change.)
5. Majority of Black Americans prefer to get news from television.
6. Black newspapers are small, community-oriented publications.
7. Black Americans are underrepresented as newsroom employees in the United States.

Consider the results of the Pew Research poll for item number four listed above. It is of note that Black Americans are possibly less concerned about made-up/fake news. The explanation for this can be explored further by looking into the historical record of the relationship between the Black community and mainstream media. Historically, many (from explorers to journalists) have created narratives that have misrepresented Black people, their society, and their culture, which could explain why Black Americans do not prioritize what is deemed made-up/fake news. This information is readily spotted for what it is—half-truth and manipulated information.

Another Pew Research poll indicates that many Black American adults felt the news media misunderstands them and for different reasons than their white and Hispanic counterparts. "Black American adults are far more likely than the other two groups to feel that the misunderstandings are based on their race or some other demographic trait."[21] But what narrative are some majority news organizations (non-black-oriented news media organizations) spinning? If it does not fit the narrative of unwed mothers on welfare, gun violence, gang violence, or looting protestors, any other story of Black America is not valid.

THE CONSERVATIVE NEWS PLAYBOOK

Since the 2016 election, much has been said and written about the bewildering affection between Evangelical Christians and Donald J. Trump. Terry Heaton, the former executive producer of The 700 Club, states that "10 years before Fox News came on the scene we, the Christian Broadcast Network (CBN), wrote the playbook for conservative news."[22] Heaton continues, "we called it T.V. News with a different spirit, and all it was, was an attempt to insert conservative propaganda into the news. In the end, right-wing news is only propaganda; it is not news. There is no attempt to be unbiased. It has gone so far now that the public does not know it."[23] It is within this media plan that the negative narrative that frames the lives of Black people, the poor, and the oppressed is normalized.

EVANGELICALS DEFINED

So, who exactly are these Evangelicals? A 2014 Pew Research Center study on religion and public life interviewed 35,000 American adults in all fifty states by phone to determine the demographic characteristics, religious beliefs and practices, and social and political views for specific religious traditions.[24] The results found that 70.6% of American adults identified as Christian with the following breakdown:

- Evangelical Protestant 25.4%
- Mainline Protestant 14.7%
- Historically Black Protestant 6.5%
- Catholic 20.8%
- Mormon 1.6%
- Orthodox Christian 0.5%
- Jehovah's Witness 0.8%
- Other Christian 0.4%

In its most concise definition, the term "evangelical" comes from the Greek word *evangel*, which refers to the good news that Jesus Christ came to save humanity. The Evangelical Christian movement historically has been defined by its members' specific doctrinal standards and practices. Yet in recent years, many Americans have come to understand Evangelicals more by their political, rather than religious, identity.[25] On the surface, this is no different from that of other mainline Protestant beliefs. But the devil is in the details. John Green, author of *Religion and Culture Wars* in an article for *PBS Frontline*,[26] lists four cardinal views that Evangelicals tend to hold:

1. The Bible is inerrant; it was and is without error in all of its claims.
2. The only way to salvation is through the Lord and Savior Jesus Christ.
3. Individuals must be converted or also known as being born-again accepting salvation for themselves; no sprinkles or dabs of water will do.
4. They must proselytize according to their fundamentalist views.

As rhetoricians, we know that denotation and etymology are only a part of the meaning words carry. Connotations are the suggested or implied meanings of a word or phrase derived over time that come to be associated with people, places, and actions beyond its literal meaning. It is precisely the connotative meaning of the words Evangelical Christian Right that carries a particular tone, a tone that evokes a specific religiopolitical ideologic narrative. That of conservativism and anti-liberation.

It was in the 1970s in response to the Civil Rights Movement that this particular brand of Christian Evangelicalism, also known as the Christian Right/ Religious Right, came into existence in the United States. The Religious Right founded and ratified its mission of segregation and oppression during this period.[27] The Christian Right or the Religious Right are Christian political factions that are characterized by their strong support of socially conservative policies. Christian conservatives seek to influence politics and public policy with their interpretation of the teachings of Christianity. White Evangelicals, who are a large part of President Donald Trump's political base, continue to glorify the privilege of the fundamentalist doctrine of manifest destiny that underlies this mission.[28] Ironically, some Evangelical Christians have differences with the current conservative right-leaning political climate. However, they remain silent or are complacent for the sake of white solidarity and maintaining the white, capitalist, patriarchal power structure. Preservation of whiteness, the founding myth of white nationalism,[29] is the priority reminiscent of times past.

The relationship between politics and religion in the United States is long-standing and contentious, dating back to the founding of the nation. The explication of it is beyond the scope and space of this chapter. Briefly, however, Christian nationalism is religion, and the separation of church and state is preached one way but practiced another, which is illustrated by the political influence that some religious groups and organizations hold in the current U.S. political process. This merging of the sacred and secular is called by some theopolitical a power espoused by Evangelical Christians and salient in these turbulent times.

DISSENTING CHRISTIAN VOICES

There are Christians who work alongside non-Christians in support of social justice and equality for the Black community and other minority groups. All have a role to play in advocating for parents and families at school board meetings, fair housing, health equity, and jobs. The dissenting voices take on many formal and informal forms of action. Highly visible civil unrest through protests, establishing and affirming equity in a professional or educational environment, and speaking up when others engage in disparaging comments and microaggressions are on the continuum of how an individual can be a dissenting voice. White Evangelicals can be a dissenting voice for inclusion, social justice, and equity.

In the spring of 1785, an itinerant Methodist preached against slavery in the Virginia countryside near Norfolk. It was a momentous occasion, pitting British native and newly minted Methodist bishop Dr. Thomas Coke against a group of lay Virginians gathered to hear the Gospel. Coke condemned slave holdings as unchristian and urged his audience to manumit[30] their slaves. Many stalked out of Brother Martin's barn, vowing to "flog" Coke as soon as he emerged. "A high-lady" egged them on, Coke reported, promising "fifty pounds, if they would give the little Doctor one hundred lashes." The threat to humiliate Coke with a punishment meant to inflict shame as well as pain on slaves came to naught finally, but the danger was palpable. The crowd dispersed only after Martin, who was the local justice of the peace as well as a Methodist convert, cornered the ringleader and talked him down.[31]

Since two-term president Barak Obama occupied the White House, some Christians and non-Christians alike have become very vocal against issues of social equity along racial, political, and religious lines. There is a fear of "socialism," access to finite resources, and the loss of privilege. A study done by McCarthy, Garand, and Olson indicates that "religion ranks among the more powerful forces driving American political polarization, sitting alongside social media, class distinctions, racial tensions," and a variety of other factors.[32] There are Christian denominations that lean a bit left and have openly voiced and affirmed their support of the Black Lives Matter movement, espouse an antiracism agenda, and espouse social justice as part of their organizational mission statements.[33]

* United Church of Christ[34]
* Presbyterian Church (USA)[35]
* American Baptist Churches

These churches are voicing ideological differences related to health care, education, income equity, and various issues of social justice and inequality—differences that make some Evangelical Christians uncomfortable as there is a cognitive dissonance that White Evangelicals must overcome to be that dissenting voice. According to Andre E. Johnson's Twitter comments in response to the White Evangelicals response to the Black Lives Matter protests:

> It is hard for those who only know white evangelical theology to talk about race or understand racism. There is nothing in their theological understanding that prepares them to deal with race. Many of them still believe in the inferiority of non-white people.[36]

Johnson continues:

For instance, to even affirm Black Lives Matter, many have to leave their faith traditions behind or begin the work or expand their theological frameworks. Because the theology/faith they have is not compatible with affirming Black Life at all.[37]

CONCLUSION: WOMANIST VOICE DISRUPTING THE NARRATIVE

As a womanist, I am concerned about and committed to the survival of an entire people.[38] The womanist tradition captures the lived experience and vocation of Black women in a variety of intersecting contexts. From mothers, entrepreneurs, educators, social workers, preachers, evangelists (in the original sense of the word), medical professionals, corporate executives, sisters, wives, to daughters, you get the point and understand that many of these roles run concurrently. Black women, African American women situate historically and contemporarily in hostile spaces in the United States of America and around the world, hostile areas that have a traumatic impact on her life and livelihood. It is the womanist tradition (an action that existed before it was named) that influences many to speak up for themselves and others. To speak out on behalf of their communities. Womanism is a tradition that seeks to force a change in the narrative on behalf of oppressed people. The advent of social media has provided alternatives for Black people and other communities of color to disseminate news and events pertaining to their communities, which can pose a challenge to traditional mainstream media even if social media is included as part of their broader communication strategy. Individuals are citizen journalists with the eyes, ears, and cell phone that have the ability to report what is happening in real time.

Katie Geneva Cannon and Ida B. Wells Barnett are two prominent women who played vital roles in disrupting the narrative of the status quo. Both were Black women living and working in hostile spaces. Both women challenged dominant power structures of oppression for the liberation of women and men. There is a community component to their work and, using the vernacular of Wells Barnett's time, "uplifting of the race." Both were the Black womanist voice in hostile spaces; for Cannon, it was during her theological education and work with the Presbyterian church, and for Wells-Barnett, it was society at large and her work as a journalist.

This antioppressionist voice will consciously and continuously speak and act out a theology of liberation that is inclusive of all humanity in a womanist tradition. If you see something, say something or do something. Womanism is for everybody.

NOTES

1. See Beverly Guy-Sheftall, *Words of Fire: An Anthology of African-American Feminist Thought* (New York: The New York Press, 1995), 23.

2. Chimamanda Ngozi Adichie. "The Danger of a Single Story" TEDGlobal July 2009 https://www.ted.com/talks/chimamanda_ngozi_adichie_the_danger_of_a_single_story?language=en.

3. Jeffrey Gottfried, et al. "Trusting the News Media in the Trump Era: Partisan Dynamics Overshadow Other Factors in Americans Evaluations of the News Media." https://www.journalism.org/2019/12/12/trusting-the-news-media-in-the-trump-era/.

4. Jerry Fallwell, Jr. Op Ed Piece in the *Washington Times*. https://www.washingtontimes.com/news/2020/apr/28/liberal-media-smears-against-liberty-university-sh/.

5. Aljazeera, https://www.aljazeera.com/programmes/listeningpost/2018/11/chosen-trump-christian-broadcasting-network-181103072226078.html.

6. Layli Phillips discusses the first use of the term *womanism* by Walker in the introduction of her anthology *The Womanist Reader*.

7. Layli Phillips discusses origins of the term *womanism*. Ogunyemi and Hudson-Weems are considered to be two of the early progenators of the term along with Walker. See The Womanist Reader p. XX.

8. Ibid.

9. Ibid.

10. Annette D. Madlock. Listening for the Call: A Reflective Essay I think I Got it Right. *Listening/Journal of Communication, Ethics, Religion, and Culture* (in press).

11. Theology of Work Project. (2013). *Calling a biblical perspective*. https://www.theologyofwork.org/uploads/general/Calling_A_Biblical_Perspective_by_the_Theology_of_Work_Project_2017.pdf.

12. Sherman, A. (2014). *The Basics of a Biblical Theology of Work*. Accessed from: https://www.thegospelcoalition.org/article/the-basics-of-a-biblical-theology-of-work/

13. Janet Woodlock, *Vocational Discernment and Female Experience of Pastoral Ministry Call* [online]. Zadok Papers, No. 231/232, Spring 2018: 8–16. Availability: <https://search.informit.com.au/documentSummary;dn=031998516466916;res=IELHSS> ISSN: 1322-0705. [cited 27 Apr 19].

14. Emnile M. Townes, *Womanist Justice, Womanist Hope* (Atlanta, GA: Scholars Press, 1993), 176.

15. Toniesha L. Taylor, Womanism, Encyclopedia of Identity, PDF, p. 5. "Womansit ethics speaks directly to the images, discourses, and actions, upheld by normative ethics, that support a racist ideology against Africana women. Womanist ethics is grounded in the daily practices and talk of women who, in their lived experiences, speak back to normative ethics that seek to discount them.

16. Katie G. Cannon. *Katie's Cannon: Womanism and the Soul of the Black Community* (New York: Continuum, 1995), 23, 56.

17. Autumn A. Arnette. Shaping the Narrative, Powered by the Black Press. National Association of Black Journalists, Journal, Winter 2017, pp. 19, 26. at www .nabj.org.

18. Black Press, community news, The Milwaukee Courier was established in 1964. https://www.loc.gov/item/sn78005245/

19. Black Press, community news, The Milwaukee Community Journal was registered in 1975. https://www.loc.gov/item/sn84025860/

20. It is important to note that media sources for news consumption differs by generation.

21. Pew Research, Jeffrey Gottfried and Michael Barthel https://www.pewresearch.org/fact-tank/2020/06/25/black-hispanic-and-white-adults-feel-the-news-media-misunderstand-them-but-for-very-different-reasons/, June 25, 2020.

22. https://www.aljazeera.com/programmes/listeningpost/2018/11/chosen-trump-christian-broadcasting-network-181103072226078.html. Contributors to this piece include: Gordon Robertson—CEO, Christian Broadcasting Network, Terry Heaton—Former executive producer, The 700 Club and author of The Gospel of Self: How Jesus Joined the GOP, Sarah Posner—Reporting fellow, The Investigative Fund and author of God's Profits: Faith, Fraud, and the Republican Crusade for Values Voters, and Nicole Hemmer—assistant professor in presidential studies, University of Virginia and author of Messengers of the Right.

23. Ibid.

24. https://www.pewforum.org/religious-landscape-study/. There is an interactive reporting tool available for data analysis.

25. Pew Research

26. Frontline the Jesus Factor. https://www.pbs.org/wgbh/pages/frontline/shows/jesus/evangelicals/evmain.html. April 29, 2004.

27. Tom Head. "The Religious Right." *ThoughtCo*. https://www.thoughtco.com/the-religious-right-721631 (accessed March 31, 2020).

28. Gregory A. Smith. "Among White Evangelicals Regular Churchgoers Are the Most Supportive of Trump." *Pew Research*. https://www.pewresearch.org/fact-tank/2017/04/26/among-white-evangelicals-regular-churchgoers-are-the-most-supportive-of-trump/.

Philip Schwadel and Gregory A. Smith. "Evangelical Approval of Trump Remains High but other Religious Groups Are Less Supportive." *Pew Research*. https://www.pewresearch.org/fact-tank/2019/03/18/evangelical-approval-of-trump-remains-high-but-other-religious-groups-are-less-supportive/.

29. Andrew L. Seidel. The Founding Myth: Why Christian Nationalism Is Un-American. (New York: Sterling, 2019).

30. Means Emancipate.

31. Extracts of the Journals of the Rev. Dr. Coke's Five Visits to America (London, 1793), 35. As cited in Sarah Barrington Gordon's The First Wall of Separation Between Church and State: Slavery and Disestablishment in Late-Eighteenth Century Virginia. *The Journal of Southern History*, 85, no. 1. (2019). file:///D:/Religious%20Right%20Evangelicals/The_First_Wall_of_Separation_b.PDF

32. Angela F. McCarthy, et al. (2019), "Religious Right, Religious Left, Both, or Neither? Understanding Religio-Political Identification." *Journal for the Scientific Study of Religion*, 58: 547–569. doi: 10.1111/jssr.12618.

33. Mark Oppenheimer, New York Times, accessed June 18, 2020 https://www.nytimes.com/2016/01/23/us/some-evangelicals-struggle-with-black-lives-matter-movement.html. (2016)

34. https://www.ucc.org/justice_racism_black_lives_matter

35. Presbyterian Church USA Advocacy and Social Justice, Accessed June 18, 2020. https://www.presbyterianmission.org/what-we-do/advocacy-social-justice/. PCUSA work on such issues as the environment, hunger and food, child advocacy, human rights, responsible investing, world peace, disaster assistance, development and grants, domestic/international public witness and social welfare.

36. Andre Johnson Twitter post 11:12 PM June 17, 2020. Twitter for IPhone.

37. Ibid Twitter post June 17, 2020. 11:25 PM Twitter or iPad.

38. Dianna L. Hayes. Standing in the Shoes My Mother Made. p. 56 in Stacey M. Floyd Thomas, Editor, Deeper Shades of Purple: Womanism in Religion and Society.

BIBLIOGRAPHY

Adichie, Chimamanda Ngozi. "The Danger of a Single Story." TEDGlobal video, filmed. 2009. https://www.ted.com/talks/chimamanda_ngozi_adichie_the_danger_of_a_single_story/recommendations/177023/share (accessed April 5, 2020).

Adney, Karley. "Womanist Theology." In *Encyclopedia of Women in Today's World: The Multimedia Encyclopedia of Women in Today's World*, edited by Mary Z. Stange, Carol K. Oyster, and Jane E. SloanFirst, 1561–1562. Thousand Oaks, CA: SAGE Publications, Inc., 2011. doi: 10.4135/9781412995962.n912.

Aljazeera. 2018. https://www.aljazeera.com/programmes/listeningpost/2018/11/chosen-trump-christian-broadcasting-network-181103072226078.html.

Arnett, Autumn. *Shaping the Narrative*. Powered by the Black Press. National Association of Black Journalists Journal. Winter (2017):19,26. https://cdn.ymaws.com/www.nabj.org/resource/resmgr/Journal_winter2017/NABJjournal-winter2017-V2.pdf.

Benson, John M. "The Polls: A Rebirth of Religion?" *Public Opinion Quarterly* 45, no. 4 (1981): 576. doi: 10.1086/268692.

Bosmajian, Haig. "The 'Wall of Separation' Metaphor in Supreme Court Church-State Decisions." *Religious Communication Today* 8 (September 1985): 1–7. https://search-ebscohost-com.ezproxy.liberty.edu/login.aspx?direct=true&db=ufh&AN=14141058&site=ehost-live&scope=site.

Braunstein, Ruth, and Malaena Taylor. "Is the Tea Party a 'Religious' Movement? Religiosity in the Tea Party versus the Religious Right." *Sociology of Religion* 78, no. 1 (Spring, 2017): 33–59. http://ezproxy.liberty.edu/login?url=https://search-proquest-com.ezproxy.liberty.edu/docview/2266344492?accountid=12085.

Byron, Gay L., and Vanessay Lovelace, eds. *Womanist Interpretations of the Bible: Expanding the Discourse*. Williston: Society of Biblical Literature. 2016. Accessed May 19, 2020. ProQuest Ebook Central.

Cannon, Katie G. "Hitting a Straight Lick with a Crooked Stick: The Womanist Dilemma in the Development of a Black Liberation Ethic." *The Annual of the Society of Christian Ethics* 7 (1987): 165–177. Accessed May 19, 2020. www.jstor .org/stable/23559475.

Cannon, Katie G., Alison P. Gise Johnson, and Angela D. Sims. "Womanist Works in Word." *Journal of Feminist Studies in Religion* 21, no. 2 (2005): 135+. *Gale General OneFile* (accessed May 19, 2020). https://link-gale-com.ezproxy.liberty .edu/apps/doc/A138812334/ITOF?u=vic_liberty&sid=ITOF&xid=a9b5feea.

Dorrien, Gary. *Economy, Difference, Empire: Social Ethics for Social Justice*. New York: Columbia University Press. Accessed May 19, 2020. doi:10.7312/ dorr14984.

Dreisbach, Daniel L. "Micah 6:8 in the Literature of the American Founding Era: A Note on Religion and Rhetoric." *Rhetoric & Public Affairs* 12, no. 1 (2009): 91–105. doi: 10.1353/rap.0.0072.

Floyd-Thomas, Stacey M. 2006. *Deeper Shades of Purple: Womanism in Religion and Society*. New York, NY: New York University Press.

Frontline The Jesus Factor. https://www.pbs.org/wgbh/pages/frontline/shows/jesus/ evangelicals/evmain.html.

Gordon, Sarah Barringer. "The First Wall of Separation between Church and State: Slavery and Disestablishment in Late-Eighteenth-Century Virginia." *Journal of Southern History* 85, no. 1 (2019): 61. *Gale Academic OneFile* (accessed April 7, 2020). https://link-gale-com.ezproxy.liberty.edu/apps/doc/A575902160/AONE?u =vic_liberty&sid=AONE&xid=91bd82ba.

Gottfried, Jeffrey, and Michael Barthel. Black, Hispanic, and White Adults Feel the News Media Misunderstands Them, but for Very Different Reasons. Pew Research Fact Tank News in the Numbers. 2020. https://www.pewresearch.org/fact-tank /2020/06/25/black-hispanic-and-white-adults-feel-the-news-media-misunderstand- them-but-for-very-different-reasons/.

Hardesty, Jared. An Angry God in the Hands of Sinners: Enslaved Africans and the Uses of Protestant Christianity in Pre-Revolutionary Boston. *Slavery & Abolition*, 35 no. 1 (2014): 66–83. doi: 10.1080/0144039X.2013.780459.

Harris, Tina M., and Rebecca J. Steiner. "Beyond the Veil: A Critique of White Christian Rhetoric and Racism in the Age of Trump." *Journal of Communication & Religion* 41, no. 1 (Spring 2018): 33–45. https://search-ebscohost-com.ezprox y.liberty.edu/login.aspx?direct=true&db=cax&AN=129779111&site=ehost-live &scope=site.

Hartmann, Douglas, Xuefeng Zhang, and William Wischstadt. 2005. "One (Multicultural) Nation under God? Changing Uses and Meanings of the Term 'Judeo-Christian' in the American Media." *Journal of Media & Religion* 4 (4): 207–234. doi: 10.1207/s15328415jmr0404_1.

Head, Tom. "The Religious Right." ThoughtCo. https://www.thoughtco.com/the- religious-right-721631 (accessed March 31, 2020).

Huckins, Kyle D. "Communication in Religious Lobbying: Making Meaning, Creating Power." *Journal of Media & Religion* 1, no. 2 (2002): 121. doi: 10.1207/ S15328415JMR0102_3.

Hughes, Ceri. "The God Card: Strategic Employment of Religious Language in U.S. Presidential Discourse." *International Journal of Communication (19328036)* 13 (January, 2019): 528–549. https://search-ebscohost-com.ezproxy.liberty.edu/login. aspx?direct=true&db=ufh&AN=139171714&site=ehost-live&scope=site.

Jackson, Ronald L., and Michael A. Hogg. "Womanism." In *Encyclopedia of Identity*, edited by Ronald L. Jackson and Michael A. Hogg, 889–893. Thousand Oaks, CA: SAGE Publications, Inc., 2010. doi: 10.4135/9781412979306.n285.

Karenga, Tiamoyo, and Chimbuko Tembo. "Kawaida Womanism: African Ways of being Woman in the World." *Western Journal of Black Studies* 36, no. 1 (Spring, 2010): 33–47. http://ezproxy.liberty.edu/login?url=https://search-proquest-com.ez proxy.liberty.edu/docview/1018074462?accountid=12085.

Kendall, Mikki. *Hood Feminism Notes from the Women that a Movement Forgot.* New York, NY: Viking, 2020.

Lunceford, Brett. "Rhetoric and Religion in Contemporary Politics." *Journal of Contemporary Rhetoric* 2, no. 2 (2012): 19–29. https://search-ebscohost-com .ezproxy.liberty.edu/login.aspx?direct=true&db=ufh&AN=79920828&site=ehost -live&scope=site.

Mannon, Bethany. Xvangelical: The Rhetorical Work of Personal Narratives in Contemporary Religious Discourse. *Rhetoric Society Quarterly*, 49, no. 2 (2019): 142–162. doi: 10.1080/02773945.2018.1547418.

Masci, David. https://www.pewresearch.org/fact-tank/2018/04/23/black-americans- are-more-likely-than-overall-public-to-be-christian-protestant/ (accessed August 13, 2020).

McCarthy, Angela F., Olson, L. R. and Garand, J. C. Religious Right, Religious Left, Both, or Neither? Understanding Religio-Political Identification. *Journal for the Scientific Study of Religion*, 58 (2019): 547–569. doi: 10.1111/jssr.12618.

Medhurst, Martin J. "Forging a Civil-Religious Construct for the 21st Century: Should Hart's 'Contract' Be Renewed?" *Journal of Communication & Religion* 25, no. 1 (2002): 86–101. https://search-ebscohost-com.ezproxy.lib erty.edu/login.aspx?direct=true&db=ufh&AN=14168163&site=ehost-live&sco pe=site.

Nelson, Thomas E., Rosalee A. Clawson, and Zoe M. Oxley. "Media Framing of a Civil Liberties Conflict and Its Effect on Tolerance." *The American Political Science Review* 91, no. 3 (1997): 567–583. *ProQuest.* Web. 8 May 2020.

Nix-Stevenson, Dara. "Womanism." In *Encyclopedia of Women in Today's World The Multimedia Encyclopedia of Women in Today's World*, edited by Mary Z. Stange, Carol K. Oyster, and Jane E. Sloan. Thousand Oaks, CA: Sage Publications 2011.

Oast, Jennifer. ""The Worst Kind of Slavery": Slave-Owning Presbyterian Churches in Prince Edward County, Virginia." *The Journal of Southern History* 76, no. 4 (2010): 867–900. Accessed April 7, 2020. www.jstor.org/stable/27919282.

Oyster and Jane E. Sloan, First ed., 1559–1560. Thousand Oaks, CA: SAGE Publications, Inc., 2011. doi: 10.4135/9781412995962.n911.

Pew Research Center. Political Polarization in the American Public. 2014. Available at <http://www.people-press.org/2014/06/12/political-polarization-in-the-americ an-public/>.

———. America's Changing Religious Landscape. 2015. Available at <http://www. pewforum. org/2015/05/12/americaschanging-religious-landscape/>. https://www.pewforum.org/2015/05/12/chapter-3-demographic-profiles-of-religious-groups/

———. Religion in Public Life. 2016. Available at http://www.pewforum.org/2016 /01/27/3-religion-in-public-life/.

_____. Religious Landscape Study. 2014. Available at https://www.pewforum.org/ religious-landscape-study/.

———. Since Trump's Election, Increased Attention to Politics—Especially among Women. 2017. Available at <http://www.people-press.org/2017/07/20/since-trumps-election-increased-attention-to-politics-especially- among-women/>.

Rodgers, Selena T. Womanism and Afrocentricity: Understanding the Intersection, *Journal of Human Behavior in the Social Environment*, 27, no. 1–2 (2017): 36–47. doi: 10.1080/10911359.2016.1259927.

Ross, Rosetta E. "Katie Geneva Cannon and the Soul of Womanism." *Journal of Feminist Studies in Religion*, 35, no. 2 (Fall 2019): 141–143. http://ezproxy.liber ty.edu/login?url=https://search-proquest-com.ezproxy.liberty.edu/docview/2359 962441?accountid=12085.

Schwadel, Philip, and Gregory A. Smith. "Evangelical Approval of Trump Remains High, but Other Religious Groups Are Less Supportive." 2019. https://www.pew research.org/fact-tank/2019/03/18/evangelical-approval-of-trump-remains-high -but-other-religious-groups-are-less-supportive/.

Seidel, Andrew L. *The Founding Myth: Why Christian Nationalism is Un-American.* New York, NY: Sterling, 2019.

Taylor, Toniesha, L. *Womanism in Ronald L. Jackson II and Michael A. Hogg Encyclopedia of Identity*. Thousand Oakes: C.A., 2010, 889–893.

Tewkesbury, Paul. "Keeping the Dream Alive: Meridian as Alice Walker's Homage to Martin Luther King and the Beloved Community." *Religion and the Arts*, 15, no. 5 (2011).

Thomas, Linda E. "KATIE CANNON: Premier Womanist Ethicist, Mentor, and Big Sister." *Journal of Feminist Studies in Religion* 35, no. 2 (Fall 2019): 145–146. http://ezproxy.liberty.edu/login?url=https://search-proquest-com.ezproxy.liberty.e du/docview/2359963459?accountid=12085.

Townes, Emilie M., Katie Geneva Cannon, and Kristine A. Culp. "Appropriation and Reciprocity in the Doing of Feminist and Womanist Ethics." *The Annual of the Society of Christian Ethics* 13 (1993): 187–203. Accessed May 19, 2020. www .jstor.org/stable/23559561.

Wilsey, John D. "'Our Country Is Destined to Be the Great Nation of Futurity': John L. O'Sullivan's Manifest Destiny and Christian Nationalism," 1837-1846." *Religions*

8, no. 4 (2017): 68. http://ezproxy.liberty.edu/login?url=https://search-proquest-com.ezproxy.liberty.edu/docview/1899748030?accountid=12085.

Wünch, Hans-Georg. "Learning from African Theologians and Their Hermeneutics: Some Reflections from a German Evangelical Theologian." *Verbum Et Ecclesia* 36, no. 1 (2015): 1–9. http://ezproxy.liberty.edu/login?url=https://search-proquest-com.ezproxy.liberty.edu/docview/1737513744?accountid=12085.

Chapter 2

A Womanist Response to Black Lives Matter and American Nationalism

Kimberly P. Johnson

On February 26, 2012, Trayvon Martin, a seventeen-year-old African American male, was walking back home from the store to the Retreat at Twin Lakes gated community in Sanford, Florida, where his father lived. He had a can of iced tea and Skittles in his hands that he had just purchased when the neighborhood "watch captain," George Zimmerman, reported Trayvon to the police as a "suspicious" person. The 911 operator advised Zimmerman to stay in his SUV and not to approach the suspicious person. Zimmerman ignored those instructions and, moments later, fired his gun, thus killing Trayvon Martin, which he claimed was in self-defense. On April 11, 2012, Zimmerman was charged with second-degree murder. By July 13, 2013, Zimmerman was found not guilty by an all-female jury that deliberated over the case for a little more than sixteen hours. On February 24, 2015, "The US Justice Department announce[d] that no federal civil rights charges will be brought against Zimmerman."[1] There are numerous vigilante deaths on black bodies that go without punishment, which keep blacks in a state of continually wondering when do black bodies get to enjoy the inalienable Rights of Life, Liberty, and the Pursuit of Happiness as described in the U.S. Declaration of Independence.

The black community viewed Trayvon Martin's death as eerily similar to the 1955 lynching of Emmett Till. Both black boys were teenagers: Trayvon was seventeen and Emmett was fourteen. Both were visiting the place where they were killed: Trayvon was visiting his father, and Emmett was visiting family in Mississippi. Ersula J. Ore argues that "neither boy whistled Vivaldi—that is, neither youth enacted tropes of whiteness to mitigate the consequences of being presumed a body 'out of place.'"[2] Both were killed after leaving a local store: Trayvon was killed walking home from the local

7–11, and Emmett was killed after buying candy from Bryant's shop. The deaths of both Emmett and Trayvon prompted social movements. Ore claims that both young men "were dubbed as sacrificial lambs—Emmett the sacrificial lamb of the civil rights movement, and Trayvon the sacrificial lamb of the Movement for Black Lives" (#BlackLivesMatter).[3] Their killers were acquitted in a court of their peers. Essentially, the only ones held responsible for the deaths of Emmett Till and Trayvon Martin were Emmett and Trayvon. They were "killed for no other reason than the fact of [their] blackness being perceived as 'threatening,' with [their] killer[s] getting away with it."[4] The black community continues to ask, when will the state stop sanctioning anti-black violence? When will black life be seen as valuable? When will the families of modern-day lynchings ever get justice for the loss of their loved ones? Ore suggests that "there is no justice for people already presumed to be disposable."[5]

In 2013, the Black Lives Matter movement was launched by three radical black organizers—Alicia Garza, Patrisse Cullors, and Opal Tometi—in response to the acquittal of George Zimmerman, Trayvon Martin's killer.[6] This movement is rooted in the "experiences of Black people who actively resist de-humanization."[7] Garza, Cullors, and Tometi claim that "Black Lives Matter is an ideological and political intervention in a world where Black lives are systematically and intentionally targeted for demise. It is an affirmation of Black folks' humanity, our contributions to this society, and our resilience in the face of deadly oppression."[8] While other organizations have used the #BlackLivesMatter to amplify anti-Black racism in North America, the Black Lives Matter (BLM) organization works to end state-sanctioned violence against black people and to end vigilante violence inflicted on black communities.[9] BLM affirms the lives of Black queer and trans folks, disabled folks, undocumented folks, folks with records, women, and all Black lives along the gender spectrum. It aims to center those who have been marginalized within Black liberation movements.

Even though BLM was not formally organized for Trayvon Martin's death, they quickly organized and were prepared for the fatal shooting that took place in Ferguson, Missouri. On August 9, 2014, Michael Brown was shot and killed in Ferguson by then-police officer Darren Wilson. In fifteen days, Darnell Moore and Patrisse Cullors organized the Black Life Matters Ride where over 600 people gathered in St. Louis to support those who were being brutalized by law enforcement (i.e., hit with rubber and wooden bullets, tear-gassed, and pepper-sprayed) and criticized by the media.[10] Michael Brown's death was the catalyst for launching the Black Lives Matter Global Network, which now has more than forty chapters.

While the BLM organization continues to expand, it still faces backlash. The Black Lives Matter movement has received the same type of criticism that was said about the Student Nonviolent Coordinating Committee (SNCC) February 1, 1960, sit-in at a Woolworth lunch counter in Greensboro, North Carolina, by four students attending North Carolina A&T State University. The sit-ins spread to five different states, and during the first three months of the sit-ins, the groups were criticized for operating autonomously and not having one specific leader.[11] Similar to SNCC, BLM's organizational pattern is more of a group-centered organization than a leader-centered group pattern. Just as members of SNCC brought their youth-led zeal to the Civil Rights Movement, BLM brings a younger energy level and sense of leadership to the current-day Civil Rights Movement. However, the main critique of BLM is that the church did not start it. According to Pastor Starsky Wilson, "The church is still caught up in trying to be the next Civil Rights Movement and believing that we have the moral authority to lead a movement. And while I agree that there is a moral authority that comes from the church . . . we cannot claim it as if we are founders, because this is a movement of the streets. It's a hip-hop movement."[12]

In their book, Amanda Nell Edgar and Andre E. Johnson centralized the agency of twenty-nine BLM members to explain the reasons and motivations behind becoming a member of the Black Lives Matter movement. A participant named "Ganda (African American, 35, Student/Research Assistant) explained that BLM means 'life.'" She elaborated, "It means life—not just us here existing—[but] us being able to live, access to good food, clean water, these are the things that living beings have. That's what Black Lives Matter means to me."[13] Another participant, "Martin (Black, 43, Activist) . . . root[ed] his definition of BLM in a quote that he attributed to Malcolm X: 'We declare the right to be a human being, to be respected by, and by any means necessary, we have to fight for these rights.'"[14] "Angela (Black, 37, Musician/Activist) located the meaning of BLM within the context of her surroundings and of her own agency. . . .. when I say, or when I hear Black Lives Matter, it means I matter. . . . Our entire culture and generation was taken from another country and brought here, and to this day we still do not get the same treatment, dogs get treated better."[15] All three participants understand the slogan Black Lives Matter to mean something different. Ganda's understanding is rooted in "life" and the ability to access our basic needs. Martin's understanding is rooted in a calling to fight for the oppressed by giving voice to the voiceless. Yet for Angela, her understanding provides affirmation to the fact that "I matter" or "she matters," her truth matters, and her experiences matter. Living in a world where one can claim that dogs are treated better than humans are, it is understandable that a person can find self-affirmation in the BLM movement, answer the calling to fight for social justice, and want to acknowledge that they deserve to have access to basic human needs.

A CRITIQUE OF #BLACKLIVESMATTER

On August 24, 2015, Barbara Reynolds wrote a derisive critique on the Black Lives Matter movement that was published in *The Washington Post*.[16] Reynolds argued that she was "trained in the tradition of Martin Luther King Jr.," as a nonviolent activist "who won hearts by conveying respectability and changed laws by delivering a message of love and unity. BLM seems intent on rejecting our proven methods. This movement is ignoring what our history has taught."[17] She claimed, "At protests today, it is difficult to distinguish legitimate activists from the mob actors who burn and loot. The demonstrations are peppered with hate speech, profanity, and guys with sagging pants that show their underwear."[18] Reynolds criticized BLM for its "questionable" strategy. She suggested, "The loving, nonviolent approach is what wins allies and mollifies enemies. However, what we have seen come out of Black Lives Matter is rage and anger."

The "questionable" strategy that Reynolds was alluding to is BLM's anti-respectability politics. The BLM movement does not subscribe to respectability politics. Evelyn Brooks Higginbotham developed the term "politics of respectability," which "assumed a fluid and shifting position along a continuum of African American resistance. The discourse . . . emphasized manners and morals while simultaneously asserting traditional forms of protest, such as petitions, boycotts, and verbal appeals to justice."[19] Allissa V. Richardson argues that the aim of respectability politics was "to be a living contradiction to the crude stereotypes of black women" as it sought to develop counter-discourses of Blackness.[20] Higginbotham explains that "adherence to temperance, cleanliness of person and property, thrift, polite manners, and sexual purity served to refute the logic behind their social subordination."[21] This particular tactic forced black women leaders into a sense of invisibility. However, anti-respectability politics did not coerce women into silence. Richardson claims, "Anti-respectability, as an approach to political communication, picks up where womanist movements of the mid-1970s left off, with intentionally radical performances of self and strong promises to value the most vulnerable Black lives. Anti-respectability asks that one bring their intersectional identity to the protest."[22] Anti-respectability politics does not require one to have to fit into any preconceived box, because individuals are invited to bring their whole selves to the BLM movement and women are not required or expected to take a back seat to leadership.

Marissa Johnson's BLM interruption of the Seattle campaign rally for presidential hopeful Senator Bernie Sanders in August 2015 is an example of "embodied discourse." She and her protest partner, Mara Willaford, "wore colorful braids and large hoop earrings purposefully on the day of their protest. She said that aesthetic . . . was really important because we wanted to represent folks who were in the 'hood. [W]e wanted to reject this notion of being respectful."[23] According to Brittney Cooper, "[e]mbodied discourse refers to a form of Black female textual activism wherein race women assertively demand the inclusion of their bodies and, in particular, working-class bodies and Black female bodies by placing them in the texts they write and speak."[24] Embodied discourse "disrupt[s] . . . the politics of respectability as the paradigmatic frames through which to engage Black women's ideas and their politics."[25] Women are using their voices and their bodies to navigate the public sphere. Embodied discourse invites womanist activists to center their own experiences and to allow those representations of self to shape their activism.

Pamela Lightsey, a womanist theologian, defended BLM activists at Boston University's Social Justice Institute in 2015 when she explained the disconnect between Black Lives Matter and the older civil rights cohort. She said BLM activists "respect the leaders of another day, but they are not going to bow down to them. They can't come into a protest march and demand a front seat or to jump on the front lines when the cameras are on. . . . The movement is not a black church initiative."[26] Lightsey also clarified why BLM does not subscribe to receiving orders from the typical heterosexual black male who sits at the top of a civil rights hierarchical model. BLM intentionally focuses on "the needs of black queers, the black transgendered, the black undocumented, black incarcerated and others who are hardly a speck on today's political agenda."[27] Rosalyn Satchel, an organizer of BLM Los Angeles, says "some BLM Los Angeles members will unapologetically tell anyone that they committed their lives to the Black liberation struggle, adopting a womanist/Black Nationalist framework, with a queer and trans lens."[28] She goes on to explain that "this is what we teach all members during orientation throughout our work."[29]

Leah Gunning Francis' womanist response to Ferguson (or BLM) is to make sure that the stories get told from the lived experiences of the people to show how different faiths can come together to support a social justice movement birthed out of tragedy. Her book, *Ferguson & Faith: Sparking Leadership & Awakening Community*, demonstrates how various faiths come together in the fight for humanity, more specifically how various womanists are fighting for the liberation and social justice of police brutality victims alongside the #BlackLivesMatter Movement.

Rev. Traci Blackmon, who self-identifies as a womanist, is ordained in both the African Methodist Episcopal (AME) Church and the United Church of Christ (UCC), is the first female to serve as senior pastor of Christ the King Church in Florissant, Missouri, and serves as the executive minister of Justice and Witness of the UCC denomination.[30] Blackmon's advocacy in Ferguson, surrounding the death of Michael Brown, Jr., was not planned. A year before the killing of Michael Brown, Blackmon had performed a funeral for a twenty-one-year-old woman killed in a drive-by shooting while holding her nine-month-old child. Blackmon is known for her funeral policy because the church offers its sanctuary to anyone who needs space to honor their deceased loved ones and they can even bring their own preacher. However, if they do not have a eulogist, then Blackmon serves the family by eulogizing the deceased.[31] A friend of the deceased, whose name is Sierra, attended the funeral and asked for Blackmon's business card after the service.[32] A year later, Sierra called upon Blackmon when she returned home from an outing with her children only to find the body of Michael Brown laying in the street. Sierra told Blackmon, "You don't know it, but since that day you've been my pastor. And, I need my pastor to come to Canfield."[33] Blackmon responded and immediately headed to the Canfield Green Apartments because Sierra needed her pastor.

Rev. Blackmon read a lot of social media posts from her clergy colleagues and later put up a post saying rather flippantly, "Well, if all we're going to do is wait and pray, can we at least do that at the police station?"[34] Immediately, people responded, asking, what time? Blackmon candidly talked about this 3:00 p.m. meeting at the police station as a "God moment" because she was able to see God bring diverse people (clergy and non-clergy) of different faiths together for a common cause.[35] She explained how she asked the clergy of various faiths to speak, but then she also admitted that she did not understand, at the time, what it meant to have so many young people surrounding them at that moment, in the midst of pain, putting aside their differences to come together and pray.[36] In hindsight, Blackmon described that moment as "a God moment that was not fully recognized because, in the midst of all of that, [she] got caught up in the message and forgot the ministry."[37] She forgot to do the ministry of drawing the pain that people were carrying into a place of healing, which is at the center of worship. From that day forward, Blackmon became a constant figure speaking at rallies, hosting community forums, and delivering speeches in various venues that speak truth to power.

WOMANISM AND THE FIGHT AGAINST
AMERICAN NATIONALISM

On January 21, 2019, Traci Blackmon delivered an address, "If These Walls Could Talk," at the St. Louis History Museum in honor of the Martin Luther King, Jr. Holiday. King (along with the Civil Rights Movement) is credited for inspiring Alice Walker to move beyond the gender gap and fight for the survival and wholeness of all people,[38] thus prompting her to redefine herself from being a feminist to (coining the term and) being a womanist. Therefore, it is never strange to reference one of the influential ancestors of the womanist movement. Furthermore, it is always appropriate to evoke the words of Dr. Martin Luther King, Jr. in a speech commemorating his birthday for the King Holiday.

Blackmon began her speech by quoting Dr. King's September 13, 1964, address, "East or West: God's Children," delivered first in West Berlin to a crowd of 20,000 people and then in East Berlin to a smaller audience of 4,000 people. The speech was three years after the Berlin Wall was built dividing the Soviet-occupied East Berlin from the U.S.-occupied West Berlin. His speech reminds us that our destiny binds us together in common humanity, common history, common calling, and common hope for the salvation of the world.[39] King's quote is as follows:

> It is indeed an honor to be in this city, which stands as a symbol of the divisions of men on the face of the earth. For here on either side of the wall are God's children and no man-made barrier can obliterate that fact. Whether it be East or West, men and women search for meaning, hope for fulfillment, yearn for faith in something beyond themselves, and cry desperately for love and community to support them in this pilgrim journey.[40]

Blackmon opens her speech with this quote from King to not only lift up the divisiveness that the Berlin Wall created between East Berlin and West Berlin but help us realize that the U.S. Border Wall is perpetuating the same type of dissention here in the United States. Blackmon recaps King's visit to Berlin by explaining to her audience that King visited a site earlier that day where border security had shot at a man more than 300 times for trying to crawl under the barbed wire fence at Checkpoint Charlie so that he could escape the communist sector of the city for the democratic sector. That man was Michael Meyer, and he survived the attack with the help of U.S. soldiers on the Western border. While there have not been many shootout incidents at the U.S. border, we can recall the brutal images plastered across the news of border patrol shooting tear gas at men, women, and children seeking asylum in the United States. President Donald J. Trump might not have been the initial architect of the Border Wall, but his signature 2016 campaign promise was to complete the wall by building a U.S.-Mexico border.

The Berlin Wall serves as a metaphor for the U.S. Border Wall, which means that King's words to East and West Berlin are applicable to the United States and Mexico. King reminds us that "on either side of the wall are God's children and no man-made barrier can obliterate that fact."[41] King was saying that regardless of our barriers, our destiny binds us together, and our common humanity makes us sensitive to each other's suffering.[42] Blackmon goes on to explain that many people were killed during the twenty-eight years the Berlin

Wall divided East and West Berlin, yet about 75,000 were able to escape. She says, "History has proven time and time again that humanity's insatiable thirst for freedom is so strong that people will risk their lives to quench it, no matter what the barriers may be. And there is no wall, neither physical or otherwise, strong enough or high enough or entrenched enough to stop those who seek freedom."[43] She admits that King's words are eerily haunting and then lifts up the fact that King "was one who dedicated his life to tearing down walls that divide humanity—on the 28th day of a partial government shutdown over funding for a border wall that holds hostage the economic safety and stability of over 800,000 furloughed federal workers who have not received a paycheck in almost 3 weeks."[44] Blackmon begins to define her metaphor by pointing out that she is really talking about the present-day divisiveness at the U.S.-Mexican border and Trump's political game to use federal workers as pawns in the scheme to shut down the government over funding for a Border Wall.

Blackmon poses rhetorical questions regarding what King might say about today's America, the state of our Union, and the failure to build bridges across political divisions. She voices a total of four questions, and in the last one, she asks, "What might he say about the building of walls—both physically and philosophically—that are increasingly becoming the ready-made solution to difference?"[45] Her answer is "America is in trouble."[46] According to Blackmon, the same pressing question that King asked in 1967, in his book *Where Do We Go From Here: Chaos or Community?*, is applicable today, and we can choose to move toward either chaos or building community.[47] Blackmon challenges her audience to "emulate his courage and conscience in the face of Empire."[48] She reminds them that King advocated for tearing down all walls, all forms of barriers both metaphorical and literal.

Blackmon critiques the current state of affairs by saying we are more concerned with winning and less concerned about advancing humanity. The United States' lack of concern centers on its need to maintain American nationalism. Blackmon reminds her audience that King even admonished his listeners to "transcend the narrow confines of nationalism" in his 1953 sermon titled, "False Gods We Worship."[49] It was in that message that King talked about "The False God of Nationalism," which affirms absolute sovereignty, white supremacy, chauvinism, and racial prejudice. Blackmon claims that nationalism cannot create community.

King is used as an example to help us understand that in order to move beyond chaos, we need a plan. Blackmon quotes King's "Beyond Vietnam" speech, where he urges America to pull out of the Vietnam War and to admit its wrongful involvement. In that speech, King was concerned with saving the soul of America. According to King, "A nation that continues year after year to spend more money on military defense than on programs of social uplift is approaching spiritual death."[50] He said, "If we are to get on the right side of the world revolution, we as a nation must undergo a radical revolution of values."[51] Blackmon talks about how King's "radical revolution of values" emphasized "Love and Justice instead of economic nationalism."[52]

Blackmon lifts up King's confession that "his conscience left him no [other] choice" but to break the betrayal of his silence on the U.S. involvement in the Vietnam War, to highlight the fact that we need to let our conscience convict us so that we too will speak truth to the powers of fear and hatred. She inquires as to how we became a nation driven by fear as opposed to faith. Blackmon answers her own question by pointing us to the Bible—Ephesians 2:14: "For he himself is our peace, who has made us both one and has broken down in his flesh the dividing wall of hostility." The goal is to get the listeners to understand that Christ's death on the cross made us one with God and broke down the dividing wall of hostility (sin) through God's forgiveness of our sins. Blackmon uses the "walls" in the scripture as well as the Berlin Wall to define our metaphorical walls that create division here in the United States. She frames the walls in the context of barriers to justice and equality by arguing:

We have built walls of indifference toward one another that prevent us from empathizing with the plight of those who don't look like us, or [sic] speak like us, or act like us—whatever that "us" may be.

We have built walls of educational inequity by funding school systems through property taxes that ensure a substandard education for those who cannot afford to live in wealthier subdivisions.

We have built walls of religious intolerance. Walls that make acceptable the lie that this country was founded upon Christian principles, as opposed to principles of capitalism cloaked in religious rhetoric.

We have built walls of economic injustice when CEOs are making more in ten minutes than some workers make a year; when a partial government shutdown is an acceptable bargaining tool because we have lost sight of 800,000 families who will be left with nothing to bargain.

We have built walls of unjust legal systems when there is absolution for those who can afford freedom and incarceration for those who cannot.

We have built walls of inefficiency when the political party one represents has become more powerful than the unifying oath to serve all the people one takes to enter public office in this country.[53]

The walls of indifference prevent us from allowing Mexican migrants to seek asylum in the United States and so we deny their entry, detain them in detentions centers where we maliciously separate children from their parents, and make the road to citizenship extremely difficult to attain. The walls of educational inequity gentrify our school systems by funneling the least amount of government funding to the most impoverished communities and the maximum amount of funding to the wealthiest communities, thus guaranteeing the best education to the more affluent students and a substandard education to the poorest students.

The walls of religious intolerance make us believe one of the myths that Richard T. Hughes talks about in his book, *Myths America Lives By: White Supremacy and the Stories that Give Us Meaning*, the "Myth of the Christian Nation," which claims that "America is a Christian nation, consistently guided by Christian values."[54] Hughes argues that the founding fathers guaranteed religious liberty and then pushed those doctrines and creeds off to the fringes of the Republic. On a minimal scale, the Declaration affirms common religious sentiments, but the Constitution only mentions religion in the First Amendment as it applies to Congress not making laws to be a respecter of religion and it intentionally fails to mention God or any other religious symbol.[55]

The walls of economic injustice that not just makes room for unequal pay across the gender line but denies access to free labor markets because wages are so low that people are unable to save for the future. These walls also allow employees to be used as pawns in a political game of chess that leaves the employees with nothing to bargain with in our free market because they were forced to go without being compensated for thirty-five days while the elected officials, who made this a reality, continued to receive their paychecks. The mere existence of this type of economic injustice is how Nancy MacLean is able to write in her book, *Democracy in Chains: The Deep History of The Radical Right's Stealth Plan for America*; about how the investigative journalist Jane Mayer was able to uncover the 2010 story on Charles and David Koch pouring more than a hundred million dollars in to the "war against Obama"; and how "other rich right-wing donors were providing vast quantities of 'dark money' (political spending that, by law, had become untraceable) to groups and candidates whose missions, if successful, would hobble unions, limit voting, deregulate corporations, shift taxes to the less well-off, and deny climate change."[56]

The walls of unjust legal systems disproportionately incarcerate black and brown bodies. The prison system seems to treat the wealthy guilty prisoners better than the poor innocent prisoners. Michelle Alexander, a former criminal attorney with the American Civil Liberties Union (ACLU), argues in her book, *The New Jim Crow: Mass Incarceration in the Age of Colorblindness*, that the criminal justice system is "not just another institution infected with racial bias but rather a different beast entirely. . . . I came to see that mass incarceration in the United States had, in fact, emerged as a stunningly comprehensive and well-disguised system of racialized social control that function in a manner strikingly similar to Jim Crow."[57] Alexander explains the parallels between the systems of social control by stating, "Once they [prisoners] are released, they are often denied the right to vote, excluded from juries, and relegated to a racially segregated and subordinated existence. Through a web of laws, regulations, and informal rules, all of which are powerfully reinforced by social stigma, they are confined to the margins of mainstream society and denied access to the mainstream economy."[58]

The walls of inefficiency derail a political party's duty to serve all people for the greater desire to control all three branches of government. This political hunger for control is what caused our elected officials to forget about their oath to serve all people as long as it guaranteed they would have a republican in the White House. That is how Donald J. Trump became the 45th President of The United States of America. "In fact," Hughes argues, "had there been no President Obama, there would never have been a President Trump."[59] When candidate Trump promised he would "make America great again," which served as not only his campaign slogan but his main campaign agenda, most blacks automatically knew what that meant—he would take back the country by reclaiming and openly welcoming the reign of white supremacy. Trump did not need political experience to get to the White House as long as he could deliver on his campaign promise of white dominance and control.

Blackmon reminds us that on both sides of these walls that act as barriers to justice and equality are children of God. She challenges us to examine our own personal walls that we erected—"[t]he divisions, the stereotypes, the scapegoating; the ease with which we blame our circumstances on others."[60] We have to self-examine the barriers we built and tear down those walls to fully participate in fighting against our common challenges—war and poverty; injustice and inequality. Next, she reveals her plan by instructing us to build bridges instead of walls because healing comes when we "dare to be vulnerable enough to be healed."[61] For Blackmon, it is not enough simply to halt the erection of new walls or to tear down walls; she urges us to build bridges:

Bridges of access to resources to fix our failing school systems.
Bridges of access to excellent and affordable healthcare so that we all can live well lives.
Bridges to citizenship that honor the contributions of all of humanity in making this country great.
Bridges to living wages for honorable work so that the economic stability of our entire region can be actualized.
Bridges to responsible criminal justice reform that reduces recidivism and promotes rehabilitation.[62]

Blackmon's plan is geared toward the wholeness and well-being of all of humanity. She fights for better school systems, the poor and middle class who are unable to afford the skyrocketing healthcare and medication costs, those who unlawfully sit in jail because they do not have enough money to afford to pay for their freedom, the migrants seeking asylum who need a clear road to citizenship, and adequate rehabilitation for criminals that will cut down on the chances of them becoming repeat offenders. Blackmon says, "We cannot allow fear to drive us to abandon a solidified front that demands equity for all of God's creation. In times of great fear and trepidation, we must resist the urge of self-preservation and boldly declare Justice can never be about 'Just-us.'"[63]

In her closing remarks, Blackmon quotes, for the last time, King's "Beyond Vietnam" speech because she believes his words are still true today:

> This, I believe to be the privilege and the burden of all of us who deem ourselves bound by allegiances and loyalties which are broader and deeper than national-ism . . . and which go beyond our nation's self-defined goals and positions.
>
> We are called to speak for the weak, for the voiceless, for the victims of our nation and for those it calls "enemy," for no document from human hands can make these humans any less our kindred.[64]

Blackmon uses the prophetic words of King, on Martin Luther King, Jr. Day, to remind us of a significant womanist value—that we are called to fight for the survival and wholeness of all people. We must advocate for those who are unable to advocate for themselves, those who have been silenced, and those who have been marginalized. At the end of her speech, we finally dis cover what the walls would say if they could talk (taken from the title of her speech, "If these walls could talk . . ."). "If these walls could talk," Blackmon proclaims, "I believe they would say history proves this true. No wall built to divide us will ever stand the test of time. From Jericho to Berlin to our Southern Borders, the walls must come down! Because on both sides of every wall, God's children are present."

CONCLUSION

In the end, will black lives, or even all of humanity, matter in the United States? Hopefully, the anti-respectability politics, along with embodied discourse, is enough to complement the womanist lens that undergirds the #BlackLivesMatter movement. Womanism propels BLM activists to use their voice and their bodies to be bold and courageous, to fight for the survival and wholeness of all people, to love themselves enough to bring their entire self to the fight for liberation and social justice, and to honor their own experiences by centering them and allowing those past experiences to shape their activism. Similarly, will a womanist perspective that privileges the experiences of the oppressed be enough to get us out of this American nationalistic chaos and move us toward building bridges by tearing down walls? Will either one be enough to put us on the right side of love and justice? My answer is yes, as long as we keep in mind that womanism demands we fight for the liberation and social justice of all oppressed people. Not just black women, but all women. Not just black people, but all people. Moreover, we must remember that womanism invites all people to participate in the fight for a better future—women, LGBTQIA, and men; the young and old; churched and unchurched, it does not matter the religion or denomination. Ultimately, time will tell.

NOTES

1. CNN Library, "Trayvon Martin Shooting Fast Facts" accessed July 18, 2019 https://www.cnn.com/2013/06/05/us/trayvon-martin-shooting-fast-facts/index.html.

2. Ersula J. Ore, *Lynching: Violence, Rhetoric, and American Identity* (Jackson: University Press of Mississippi, 2019), 130.

3. Ore, *Lynching*, 132.

4. Kelly Brown Douglass, *Stand Your Ground: Black Bodies and the Justice of God* (Maryknoll: Orbis Books, 2015), viii.

5. Ore, *Lynching*, xiv.

6. Black Lives Matter, "Herstory" accessed September 7, 2018 https://blacklivesmatter.com/about/herstory/.

7. Equal Justice Society, "Black Lives Matter and Alicia Garza," *Equal Justice Society*, accessed July 22, 2019 https://equaljusticesociety.org/Blacklivesmatter/.

8. Black Lives Matter, "Herstory," accessed September 7, 2018 https://black-livesmatter.com/herstory/.

9. Ibid.

10. Ibid.

11. Paula Giddings, *When and Where I Enter: The Impact of Black Women on Race and Sex* (New York: William Morrow, 1984), 274.

12. Leah Gunning Francis, *Ferguson & Faith: Sparking Leadership & Awakening Community* (St. Louis: Chalice Press, 2015), 111.

13. Amanda Nell Edgar and Andre E. Johnson, *The Struggle over Black Lives Matter and All Lives Matter* (Lanham: Lexington Books, 2018), 8.

14. Ibid., 9.

15. Ibid., 10.

16. Barbara Reynolds, "I Was a Civil Rights Activist in the 1960s. But It's Hard for Me to Get Behind Black Lives Matter," *Washington Post*, August 24, 2015,

accessed July 22, 2019 https://www.washingtonpost.com/posteverything/wp/2015/0
8/24/i-was-a-civil-rights-activist-in-the-1960s-but-its-hard-for-me-to-get-behind-bla
ck-lives-matter/.

17. Barbara Reynolds, "I Was a Civil Rights Activists."

18. Ibid.

19. Evelyn Brooks Higginbotham, *Righteous Discontent: The Women's Movement
in Black Baptist Church, 1880–1920* (Cambridge: Harvard University Press,
1993), 187.

20. Allissa V. Richardson, "Dismantling Respectability: The Rise of New
Womanist Communication Models in the Era of Black Lives Matter" *Journal of
Communication*, March (2019), 3.

21. Evelyn Brooks Higginbotham, *Righteous Discontent*, 193.

22. Richardson, "Dismantling Respectability," 16.

23. Richardson, "Dismantling Respectability," 15.

24. Brittney C. Cooper, *Beyond Respectability: The Intellectual Thought of Race
Women* (Urbana: University of Illinois Press, 2017), 3.

25. Ibid.

26. Barbara Reynolds, "I Was a Civil Rights Activists."

27. Ibid.

28. Rosalyn Satchel, Personal communication to author, January 15, 2020.

29. Ibid.

30. Jack Jenkins, "This Missouri Pastor Is Working to 'Reclaim the Language of
Faith'" *ThinkProgress*, November 13, 2017, accessed March 20, 2018 https://thinkpr
ogress.org/rev-traci-blackmon-c81f140e144f/.

31. Ibid.

32. Ibid.

33. Ibid.

34. Francis, *Ferguson & Faith*, 24.

35. Ibid.

36. Ibid., 25.

37. Ibid., 26–27.

38. Alice Walker, *In Search of Our Mother's Garden: Womanist Prose* (Orlando:
Harcourt Inc., 1983), 124–125.

39. Martin Luther King Jr., "East or West: God's Children," *Inside the Cold War:
Marx to Reagan: An Unprecedented Guide to the Roots, History, Strategies, and Key
Documents of the Cold War* (Lanham: University Press of America, 2015), accessed
January 7, 2020. http://insidethecoldwar.org/reference-materials/documents

40. Traci Blackmon, "If These Walls Could Talk," *United Church of Christ*,
January 21, 2019, accessed March 24, 2019. https://www.ucc.org/commentary_trac
i_blackmon_if_these_walls_could_talk_01212019.

41. Ibid., See also, Martin Luther King Jr., "East or West:God's Children."

42. King, "East or West: God's Children."

43. Blackmon, "If These Walls Could Talk."

44. Ibid.

45. Ibid.

46. Ibid.
47. Ibid.
48. Ibid.
49. Ibid.
50. Clayborne Carson and Kris Shepherd, eds., *A Call to Conscience: The Landmark Speeches of Dr. Martin Luther King, Jr* (New York: Warner Books, 2001), 159.
51. Clayborne Carson and Kris Shepherd, eds., *A Call to Conscience*, 157.
52. Blackmon, "If These Walls Could Talk."
53. Ibid. (italics added).
54. Richard T. Hughes, *Myths American Lives By: White Supremacy and the Stories that Give Us Meaning* (Urbana: University of Illinois Press, 2018), 2.
55. Ibid., 83.
56. Nancy MacLean, *Democracy in Chains: The Deep History of the Radical Right's Stealth Plan for America* (New York: Viking, 2017), xvii; See also Jane Mayer, "Covert Operations: The Billionaire Brother Who Are Waging a War against Obama," *The New Yorker*, August 30, 2010; and, more recently, Jane Mayer, *Dark Money: The Hidden History of the Billionaires behind the Rise of the Radical Right* (New York: Doubleday, 2016).
57. Michelle Alexander, *The New Jim Crow: Mass Incarceration in the Age of Colorblindness* (New York: The New Press, 2010), 4.
58. Ibid.
59. Hughes, *Myths American Lives By*, 117.
60. Blackmon, "If These Walls Could Talk."
61. Ibid.
62. Ibid. (italics added).
63. Ibid.
64. Ibid.

BIBLIOGRAPHY

Alexander, Michelle. *The New Jim Crow: Mass Incarceration in the Age of Colorblindness*. New York: The New Press, 2010.

"Black Lives Matter and Alicia Garza." Equal Justice Society. Accessed July 22, 2019. https://equaljusticesociety.org/Blacklivesmatter/.

"BLM Los Angeles." Black Lives Matter. Accessed July 23, 2019. https://blackli vesmatter.com/chapter/blm-los-angeles/.

Blackmon, Traci. "If These Walls Could Talk." *United Church of Christ*. January 21, 2019. https://www.ucc.org/commentary_traci_blackmon_if_these_walls_coul d_talk_01212019.

Carson, Clayborne, and Kris Shepherd, eds., *A Call to Conscience: The Landmark Speeches of Dr. Martin Luther King, Jr.* New York: Warner Books, 2001, 159.

Cooper, Brittney C. *Beyond Respectability: The Intellectual Thought of Race Women*. Urbana: University of Illinois Press, 2017.

Douglass, Kelly Brown. *Stand Your Ground: Black Bodies and the Justice of God*. Maryknoll: Orbis Books, 2015.

Edgar, Amanda Nell, and Andre E. Johnson. *The Struggle over Black Lives Matter and All Lives Matter*. Lanham: Lexington Books, 2018.

Francis, Leah Gunning. *Ferguson & Faith: Sparking Leadership & Awakening Community*. St. Louis: Chalice Press, 2015.

Giddings, Paula. *When and Where I Enter: The Impact of Black Women on Race and Sex*. New York: William Morrow, 1984.

"Herstory." Black Lives Matter. Accessed September 7, 2018. https://blacklivesmatter.com/herstory/.

Higginbotham, Evelyn Brooks. *Righteous Discontent: The Women's Movement in Black Baptist Church, 1880 – 1920*. Cambridge: Harvard University Press, 1993.

Hughes, Richard T. *Myths America Lives By: White Supremacy and the Stories that Give Us Meaning*. Urbana: University of Illinois Press, 2018.

Jenkins, Jack. "This Missouri Pastor Is Working to 'Reclaim the Language of Faith.'" *ThinkProgress* (November 13, 2017). Accessed March 20, 2018. https://thinkprogress.org/rev-traci-blackmon-c81f140e144f/.

King, Jr., Martin Luther. "East or West: God's Children." In *Inside the Cold War: Marx to Reagan: An Unprecedented Guide to the Roots, History, Strategies, and Key Documents of the Cold War*. Lanham: University Press of America, 2015. Accessed January 7, 2020. http://insidethecoldwar.org/reference-materials/documents

MacLean, Nancy. *Democracy in Chains: The Deep History of the Radical Right's Stealth Plan for America*. New York: Viking, 2017, xvii.

Ore, Ersula J. *Lynching: Violence, Rhetoric, and American Identity*. Jackson: University Press of Mississippi, 2019.

Reynolds, Barbara. "I Was a Civil Rights Activist in the 1960s. But It's Hard for Me to Get Behind Black Lives Matter." *Washington Post* (August 24, 2015), Accessed July 22, 2019. https://www.washingtonpost.com/posteverything/wp/2015/08/24/i-was-a-civil rights-activist-in-the-1960s-but-its-hard-for-me-to-get-behind-black-lives-matter/.

Richardson, Allissa V. "Dismantling Respectability: The Rise of New Womanist Communication Models in the Era of Black Lives Matter." *Journal of Communication*, (March 2019): 3.

"Trayvon Martin Shooting Fast Facts." *CNN* online. Last modified January 10, 2020. https://www.cnn.com/2013/06/05/us/trayvon-martin-shooting-fast-facts/index.html.

Walker, Alice. *In Search of Our Mother's Garden: Womanist Prose*. Orlando: Harcourt Inc., 1983.

Chapter 3

Examining Grace Greenleaf

Black Women's Activism and Spirituality

Cerise L. Glenn

Greenleaf, a television drama on the Oprah Winfrey Network (OWN), centers the Greenleaf family, a prominent African American family heading Calvary, a major megachurch in the Southeastern United States. *Greenleaf* aired for five seasons from 2016–2020. Due to the show's popularity, it is also available on Netflix. The Greenleaf family is headed by Bishop James and Lady Mae Greenleaf, the pastor and first lady of the Calvary church. The show begins with the return of their eldest daughter of four children, Grace, who creates tension as she works to unearth secrets regarding her family and the church as she copes with the loss of her sister, Faith. Jacob and Charity, her other two siblings, also reside in the Greenleaf residence with their parents, spouses, and children.[1] All members of the family occupy important roles at Calvary, making it mostly a family-run church. The plotlines of the show feature stories centering church dynamics and leadership, adultery, sibling rivalry, among others. The family negotiates difficult tensions of family, faith, and public church roles throughout the series. Additionally, tensions between members of Calvary regarding policing and additional social justice issues are examined in the first seasons.

One of the interesting aspects of *Greenleaf* regards major plotlines centering on the role of women in the family and at Calvary. Grace Greenleaf, the main character, is portrayed as a strong-willed, opinionated single mother who returns to her family after living away from them for several years when her sister, Faith, passes away. With a lead storyline featuring African American women and issues regarding faith and family, tenets of womanism and Black feminist thought serve as useful frames for explicating portrayals of contemporary women in the church. More specifically, this chapter examines Grace Greenleaf's efforts to support women in the church and advocate for social justice through the tenets of womanism and Black feminist thought.

Her successes and difficulties reflect tensions Black women experience in their families and church communities as they challenge marginalizing discourses of Black womanhood.

AFRICAN AMERICAN WOMEN'S SPIRITUALITY AND THE BLACK CHURCH: WOMANISM AND BLACK FEMINIST THOUGHT

Womanism centers African American female culture, with its commitment to survival and emotional strength.[2] Alice Walker, credited with creating the term "womanism," explains it as "A black feminist or feminist of color. From the black folk expression of mothers to female children, 'You acting womanish,' i.e., like a woman. Usually referring to outrageous, audacious, courageous, or *willful* behavior" (p. xi).[3] Walker addresses how African American women can actively challenge the oppressive forces in their lives, particularly the intersections of racism, sexism, classism, sexual orientation, in addition to other aspects of social identity.[4] As noted by Walker, womanism and Black feminism are interconnected.[5] Patricia Hill Collins, who is often credited with explicating the theoretical framework of Black feminism, describes Black feminist thought as a critical social theory that also centers on Black women's lived experiences from an intersectional perspective.[6] Like womanism, Black feminism creates a framework for examining how women of color challenge oppressive experiences and forces in their lives. The role of Black feminism is also rooted within a broader feminist agenda to address and resolve systemic issues in major societal institutions, particularly economic, political, social, and educational ones,[7] Both womanism and Black feminism focus on the agency of Black women, as well as other marginalized groups, by emphasizing how self-definition and collective action can challenge oppression.

Although womanism and Black feminism share congruent aims, they can differ in focal points to achieve these aims. Womanism centers holism and spirituality. Sandra Schneiders defines *spirituality* as "the experience of striving to integrate one's life in terms of self-transcendence toward the ultimate value one perceives."[8] As such, womanism has a theological vein that centers on Black women's experiences with their spirituality, particularly in connection to religious beliefs and the organizational structure of Black churches. The role of Black women in churches has a complicated tension of marginalization and empowerment. Historically, Black churches have served as a vital component of community building and support. Churches provide outreach programs essential for the livelihood of its members and their surrounding communities. These include outreach and programs regarding child development, elderly services, family support, among others.[9] The role of women in churches has been more problematic despite the beneficial aspects of Black churches.[10] For instance, womanist and Black Feminist scholars explain that they still encounter aspects of sexism as they learn to navigate the politics of respectability and acceptability.[11] This can manifest through challenges of Black women in leadership roles in the church, with some church members believing that the role of leadership belongs exclusively to heterosexual males.[12] For example, Julia Foote argues that some male Christians believe women pretend to receive the Divine call, and unless they show their "credentials" from heaven, they will continue to doubt the authenticity of their call.[13]

Melanie C. Jones explains that Black women feel pressured to dress in more conservative ways in order to be viewed as respectable by their African American and white counterparts, illustrating how it can become a central aspect of everyday experiences Black women encounter in churches.[14] This pressures them to "regain their moral virtue" in the public eye and in the eyes of the church. It then creates and reinforces the perception that women who dress "inappropriately" aren't "fit" for leadership roles in Black churches, creating a very limited, constraining space for Black women to occupy. Many women, and men, internalize these norms and create a self-surveilling culture where they begin to equate conservative attire with acceptability and police their own bodies in addition to other members of their congregations. Jones contends that from a womanist perspective, Black women must learn to love themselves for who they are more so than focusing on societal perceptions of them.[15] Consistent with the self-definition tenet of Black feminist thought,[16] African American women can use their own self-perceptions to challenge marginalizing perceptions of others that deem them less acceptable.

BLACK WOMEN IN LOVE AND IN TROUBLE: THE NEED FOR "SAFE" SPACES

Grace Greenleaf works to foster agency, empowerment, and voice to African American women, both through her role as associate pastor and quietly through informal channels. These efforts are part of her struggle to redeem the passing of her sister, Faith, who was sexually abused by their uncle, Mac. She immediately answers this call when she is appointed associate pastor in the first season through creating Sisters of Tamar, a support group for women in domestic violence situations and women who have been sexually abused. The creation of her group is met with both welcome and criticism at Calvary. The group becomes popular very quickly, despite critique that such a dark topic does not belong in the church. Grace's work speaks to the womanist notion of Black women being "in love and in trouble," as espoused by Alice Walker[17] through the creation of a "safe space" as discussed in Black feminist

thought.[18] Walker and Collins discuss the bind Black women face in relationships, particularly in heterosexual relationships with Black men. Black
women often view African American institutions, such as churches and mar-
riages, as safe spaces because they can foster racial solidarity and communal-
ism.[19] Although these institutions can foster love, they also create trouble due
to the pain Black women can endure working to support their communities
and partners when they must negotiate oppressive relationships mired by
sexism at the hands of men experiencing the pain of being oppressed due
to racism.[20] Therefore, these spaces some women believe to be safe may be
more troublesome, as they end up sharing them with African American males
who may have a vested interest in maintaining one or more forms of women's
oppressive conditions.

The storyline of the character Stacy reflects the tension between love
and trouble relationships and how Grace extends beyond the community
of care in the Black church to more systemic support for women, particularly African American female church members. Stacy, one of the women
attending Grace's support group, discusses patterns of repeated abuse at
the hands of Black men. She discusses being assaulted in her youth by one
of her mother's boyfriends, and her husband's abuse is also later revealed.
When Stacy shows up in Grace's office with a black eye at the hand of
her husband, Grace tries to help Stacy leave her situation by staying at a
shelter. Unfortunately, the shelter is unable to accommodate her, and Grace
puts Stacy and her children up in a hotel room for the evening. Once at the
hotel, they discuss the abuse and Stacy explains her husband struck her out
of anger because she shared her prior abuse with the other women participating in the church support group. He was embarrassed by her sharing the
story with other church members and wants her to stop attending group
meetings. He hit her because she does not want to stop participating in the
group. As Stacy and Grace continue to discuss her options, Grace advises
her not to go back to her husband until he gets help for being abusive.
Stacy replies that she will go back to him because she does not want her
two daughters to grow up without a father in the household. Stacy's story
reflects how love and trouble relationships manifest for women married
with children, as well as how seemingly safe spaces may also work against
each other when one is entrenched with abuse (or other forms of gendered
oppression).[21] This further reflects how her sense of spirituality is grounded
more in valuing her husband's wishes at the expense of her own well-being.
Stacy's decision to put her husband above her own needs reflects how Black
women feel pressured to adhere to more traditional notions of femininity,
such as passivity and submission to their husbands.[22] In this instance, two
safe spaces—the institution of marriage and the church—do not function to
protect and support Black women. Stacy's attempt at agency, a key aspect

of empowerment, is thwarted by her husband, who should also function as a type of safe space for her.[23] Despite this, the support group Grace creates shows how safe spaces are needed for women *within* the safe space in church communities.

BLACK WOMEN'S SOCIAL JUSTICE: THE POLITICS OF RESPECTABILITY AND SILENCE

An overarching storyline in Greenleaf centers Grace's decision to stay with her family to bring her uncle, Mac, to justice for abusing her sister, Faith. In addition to creating Sisters of Tamar, Grace works tirelessly to remove Mac from his position of working with legal and financial matters of Calvary in an effort to bring him to justice legally. She also works to expand her Sisters of Tamar support group to start a legal fund for women who have been abused. This line of work highlights social justice inequities for abused women and ways women's voices are silenced in Black churches. As Chaney describes, some male church leaders use their power to take advantage of congregation members.[24] They use their position in the church to mitigate their wrongdoings because they are viewed as redeemable, good God-fearing men. Mac attempts to thwart Grace's efforts and avert his responsibility, an aspect of hegemonic masculinity that men use to maintain their social power.[25] He does this by multiple means: utilizing his position of power to silence and intimidate the women in the church, including open threats to Grace; using the church scholarship fund to silence girls in socially disadvantaged positions; and using the power of his relationship with his sister, Lady Mae Greenleaf, the first lady of the church, to his advantage.

Refusing to be swayed by Mac's attempts to silence her, Grace continues her pursuit using her own position in the church to encourage the girls and their mothers. Contemporary womanists discuss how Black women have worked hard to achieve more prominence in leadership roles in the church. Womanist spirituality is important to the Black church, because it connects the viewpoint of marginalized and oppressed individuals.[26] By being a Black woman, Grace is able to recognize and help with issues that Black girls and women face. Although the girls and mothers Grace speaks to are initially afraid and hesitant to speak to her, they eventually share details of Mac's abuse. In this process, Grace discovers he has been scaring and bribing the girls he has assaulted for several years. She learns that Darlene, her administrative assistant and long-time member of Calvary, is the mother of one of the girls Mac sexually assaulted and that her daughter received scholarship funds for her silence. When Grace and Darlene discuss Mac's abusive history, Darlene vehemently apologizes and feels shamed by her silence as she hoped she would find a way to move past it so she would not have to leave her church home.

Grace continues to mount more evidence about Mac's multiple attacks on young women. When confronted, Mac vehemently denies the accusations and appeals to his sister, Lady Mae, to advocate for him. He tells her the girls are lying about being assaulted and attempts to justify the use of scholarship funds. Mac tells Lady Mae that he never disclosed these situations because he did not want the girls' lies to tear them apart. He further asserts that these girls targeted him because he has a good heart, as well as access to money and power. He denies sexually abusing Faith when Lady Mae asks and, after denying it, tells her, "It's a crime that Faith is not here and GiGi (Grace) is still here to trouble you."[27] Mac's framing of women as the problem causing his troubles reflects the power dynamics that disadvantage women. It further reflects how Mac is able to rely upon the "politics of respectability" to further marginalize the young women he abuses. The politics of respectability has been used to silence and oppress Black women in churches and larger society.[28] This is not a contemporary phenomenon for Black women. Richardson explains that during the post-Reconstruction era, Black Baptist female activists functioned under the ideology of the white gaze, trying to assimilate to the norms of whiteness and Victorian notions of womanhood.[29] As activism progressed in Black churches, the leadership of unmarried Black mothers, queer Black people, and other Black cultural groups continued to be suppressed during the Civil Rights Movement. For example, Claudette Colvin, an unmarried teenage mother and the original initiator of the 1955 Montgomery Bus boycott, was not supported as the face of civil rights. She refused to give up her seat nine months before Rosa Parks; however, Rosa Parks, who was a married, churchgoing, seamstress, was uplifted instead because she fit into the norm of acceptability.[30] The politics of respectability further convinces women who adhere to it to value themselves by their appeal to men. They must be "marriage worthy."

Moultrie explains that the Black church had embedded the notion of "living a holy and sanctified life" into the minds of Black women, meaning that they must refrain from sexual activity until after they are married and dress in conservative attire to be "ladylike."[31]: She further asserts that some religious leaders, for instance in their regular sermons, instruct Black women to "act like a wife" so that they can get a husband. In *Greenleaf*, Mac preys upon young women in desperate need of financial support and approval from a "respectable" man in the church. He uses his power and prominence to discredit the women and even blame them for his abuse. Despite this, Grace gathers enough evidence against Mac to bring him to justice through his removal of his position at church and in the criminal justice system. She consults with a police officer and reporter to find proof of Mac's abuse and press formal charges that lead to his incarceration. Her efforts reflect that women have power and agency in systems stacked against them, although it comes at great expense and they may have to utilize networks outside of their church communities. For Grace, this means a problematic relationship with her mother and the decision to leave the family when she was younger to escape abuse. After Mac is arrested and details of years of his assaults on young women in the church come to light, Grace hesitantly agrees to preach to the dwindling congregation for a summer. At the beginning of her first sermon in this role, she asks for a moment of silence for the women Mac assaulted and for others who are also suffering from abuse. As the audience observes the moment of silence, she states that the silence ends today and references many hard conversations that will need to be had as the church heals.

After Grace is able to have her uncle, Mac, removed from the church and arrested, her continued support of women reflects how sexism and silencing of women have become systemic and institutionalized. For instance, the long-standing bias against women also manifests when Grace uses the legal fund to obtain counsel for Coralie Hunter, a white woman who killed her abusive husband in self-defense. Coralie must make the agonizing decision to take a plea or go to trial. The district attorney visits Grace at her office to discuss Coralie's case. He tells Grace to convince Coralie to plead guilty and she will only serve twenty years. He states, "I mean . . . pardon me for saying this. I know this is a righteous time for ladies [referencing social protests like the #metoo movement]. But Grace, I swear, it's starting to look like you think women should be able to take the law into their own hands and kill men. That just doesn't seem right, legal, or very Christian. Have Mrs. Hunter take the deal."[32] Grace convinces Coralie to fight the charges, which are ultimately dismissed. Although this situation ends with a more positive result, it reflects hegemonic perceptions regarding women's ability to stand up for themselves and subjugate their needs to men. As the series progresses, Grace continues to be socially punished and professionally threatened for her work advocating for women's agency and empowerment.

INTRAGROUP DYNAMICS: TENSIONS OF SUPPORT AND DIVISIVENESS IN BLACK LIVES MATTER

Although womanism focuses on Black women, the communities in which they live are also a significant aspect of their experiences. The first season of *Greenleaf* features a storyline regarding police brutality, specifically procedural (in)justices by police killing African Americans—a very problematic and traumatic reality for many African American communities. David Nelson, a Black police officer, shoots and kills Kenny Collins, a

young African American male. Grace, in her role as associate pastor, decides
to assist David Nelson, who may be facing charges pertaining to Collins'
death. This issue parallels real-life issues in African American communities,
as evidenced by the Black Lives Matter social movement protesting police
brutality. Black Lives Matter became popularized after the deaths of Trayvon
Martin and Michael Brown, African American males shot and killed (the former by a private citizen acting as community law enforcement and the latter
by a police officer). In both instances, the men who shot the young African
American males were acquitted or not charged, which was perceived as an
outrageous miscarriage of justice by many African American communities
and allies. After Brown was shot and killed in 2014 in Ferguson, Missouri,
the movement gained more momentum and visibility in the public eye. Social
injustice issues regarding policing African Americans and systemic racism
and violence in Black communities grew to a more national and global movement in 2020, regenerating awareness and involvement with Black Lives
Matter. On May 25, 2020, George Floyd, an African American man, was
brutally murdered by police in Minneapolis, Minnesota. Mobile phone video
coverage shows a white male police officer kneeling on Floyd's neck while
he was handcuffed face down on the street for close to nine minutes. Despite
his cries of "I can't breathe" and other obvious signs of distress, other police
officers watched as he pleaded for his life. Floyd's death has spurred calls for
justice and holding police accountable for deaths of other African Americans,
including Breonna Taylor, as well as lack of justice for African Americans
killed by white Americans deeming themselves community patrollers of
suspected criminals who are innocent, such as Ahmaud Arbery, who was
killed while jogging by three white men who racially profiled him in his own
neighborhood. As a movement, Black Lives Matter functions as a relatively
open, loose, and inclusive network working on these important social justice
issues and advocating for change as well as accountability.[33]

Calvary's conflicted and reticent involvement regarding their church
member, David Nelson, an African American police officer, reflects nuances
and intragroup differences within African American communities regarding
police violence and perceptions of social justice. When examining African
American communities, popular culture and research can regard them as a
monolith, presuming a sameness within African American culture that does
not take into consideration how African Americans can vary within groups
and in different societal roles.[34] Womanism provides a frame for how this
can occur along the line of gender dynamics in addition to the power of
patriarchy in the church. Bishop Greenleaf initially ignores Nelson's calls
for assistance; however, Grace builds a relationship with Nelson against her
father's wishes not to get involved with this matter. The Bishop finds himself
in a moral and political predicament as Black churches are a central vein of

activism in efforts regarding Black Lives Matter, yet he has been asked to counsel and support an officer charged with an offense that is central to the cause. Furthermore, the Black Lives Matter protests calling for social justice for Kenny Collins are being led by a pastor at Triumph, a rivalry church of Calvary. Bishop Greenleaf has opted not to make a public statement regarding the death of Kenny Collins or address calls for David Nelson's arrest. Grace chooses to favor the side of spiritual counseling for Nelson since he is a member of Calvary. While not going public with support, Grace contacts Nelson privately and asks if he wants guidance while he awaits the decision on being criminally charged.

Although Nelson admits his lawyer advised him to reach out to Bishop Greenleaf because it would look good for him to have the Bishop present at a press conference, his later interactions with Grace reflect his spiritual turmoil. Grace fulfills one of the church's mission to provide spiritual counseling to him, even though it becomes more controversial and creates tensions within the leadership of the church. Grace chooses her own definition of what is spiritually correct instead of working within the power dynamics of Calvary, which privilege her father, Bishop Greenleaf, as well as other church leaders. As Jones explains, Grace is learning to define her spirituality and how this should be enacted in her own terms.[35] This provides a means to challenge the patriarchal structure of Calvary, while also working to advance the mission of the church. As she is learning this process, she does so in secrecy and hesitation. Instead of openly admonishing her when he learns of her actions, Bishop Greenleaf advises Grace to be careful about how she goes against his wishes of getting involved, while giving him the impression she was respecting his decision. Bishop Greenleaf tells her, "The right thing to do is to do what you said you was gonna do. Let your yesses be yes and your nos be no, Gigi. Otherwise folks won't know who the heck you are. Most notably you."[36] The Bishop's advice to stand in strength on her decisions not only reinforces her own decisions regarding her spiritual calling but also shows how men can support women with love in the process.

David Nelson's storyline also complicates and adds nuance to larger societal issues impacting African American communities, such as Black Lives Matter, because he is an *African American* police officer and a member of a Black church. As previously noted, Black churches are integral parts of Black communities in terms of support and activism. Schools, police departments, hospitals, and local prisons are some of the agencies that churches work with to sponsor community outreach programs.[37] Most instances of Black deaths by the hand of police officers in the public eye have been at the hands of *white* officers. This instance, centering an African American male, highlights intragroup dynamics of power and inclusion, in addition to centering the role of women and spirituality within this tension.

The intragroup dynamics are further complicated at an organizational and leadership level of the church's activism and work for social justice. Furthermore, the tension between religion and secularism is ingrained in American ideology and often has overlapping discourses about race in the United States.[38]

With Black Lives Matter, the emphasis of protestors centers the wronged party, typically an African American male. The church Triumph, and other members of the community, hold protests advocating for Collins and for formal charges to be brought against Nelson. Calvary's leadership reflects divisiveness as they are both encouraged to show support for Nelson, the Black officer, and also be an active part of restoring the police force's image in Black communities, while also supporting Black Lives Matter. The local mayor approaches the Bishop to have an African American megachurch engage in a show of support for police officers in a "Back the Blue Day." Although the Bishop has mixed feelings on this, he ultimately decides to have the event. Members of the deacon's board, however, disagree with his decision to look like they are supporting a mostly white police force, who have disproportionately injured and killed African Americans, despite Nelson's racial and ethnic background and membership at Calvary.

Some religious activists assert that the Black church struggles with being a primary site for social justice and activism in contemporary social movements, which are often considered movements of the street and/or a hip hop generation that is not closely tied to religious organizations.[39] For womanists, this creates a tension between maintaining a communal ethic of care that centers spirituality and also meeting current needs of communities who have distanced themselves from Black churches. On the day of "Back the Blue Day," Bishop is in the pulpit telling the congregation about the tragic incident with David Nelson and Kenny Collins. He also tells the congregation that Nelson is sitting in the audience. Bishop Greenleaf begins to shout, "Black lives matter. Black loves matter. Black laughs matter. Black tears matter."[40] As the choir begins to sing, multiple police officers, mostly white, come to the stage behind the pulpit to shake the Bishop's hand. Congregation members, including deacons, began to walk out of the church as this transpires. This reflects that the sense of community extends beyond racial solidarity to issues of systemic injustices. It reflects how there are times when Black churches will not support other African Americans; their disdain for the institution of the police force carries more weight than racial solidarity with Nelson, showing that members of the community see him as part of the problem as a police officer regardless of race.[41] The split within the Calvary congregation shows the tension between spirituality and care, as espoused in womanism, and challenging larger institutional oppression, an element of Black feminist thought, as represented through the showcasing of the mostly white police force.

NAVIGATING SPIRITUALITY IN ROMANTIC
AND FAMILIAL RELATIONSHIPS

Grace Greenleaf utilizes her public role in the church to obtain justice for her sister, Faith, and other abused women. She also plays an important role in getting Calvary to take a stance, albeit a highly controversial one, regarding police and social justice. Her personal life, however, occurs primarily behind "closed doors" and is great source of internal tension as she struggles with morals and spirituality. Her relationship with the fathers of her two children and her romantic interest, Darius, function as important aspects of her story-line in *Greenleaf.* This is especially significant because she has never been married or plans to be married, and her two children are fathered by different men, which violates the norm of "acceptable" relationships for Black women in the church. As noted with the politics of respectability, women are often taught that marriage is their desirable relationship goal. Society and the Black church often make Black women feel that they must get married in order to be viewed as respectful.[42] This is a church and societal norm that Grace openly and repeatedly rejects throughout the *Greenleaf* series.

In the opening season, Grace has difficulty managing her romantic feelings for Noah, the head of security of Calvary, who lives in a separate residence on the Greenleaf property. Grace and Noah were romantically involved as teenagers until Grace left home. When Grace returns several years later, Noah is engaged. The two still have feelings for each other but try to keep their relationship more plutonic while Noah assists Grace with finding evidence regarding her uncle, Mac. As they continue to work together, their old feelings begin to resurface. They both reveal they still love each other and spend the night together. Despite this, the two do not rekindle their relationship and Noah marries his fiancé. Although Grace and Noah engage in sexual activity outside of marriage, which Noah is not engaging in with his fiancé at the time due to her beliefs, the consequences for the effect this has on Noah and his new wife are not included in part of the plotline of the show as the newly wedded couple moves across the country. Unlike most of the stories in Walkers' love and trouble collection, Grace and Noah's relationship is characterized by one of love and support and Noah functions as a safe space for her.[43] During their night together, Grace tells Noah, "You were home to me. When I was with you, I was home. He (Mac) took that away from me, along with everything else. I hate him for that."[44] A religious leader's actions can significantly impact the lives of those around them.[45] Her leaving home to escape potential, and likely, sexual abuse from her uncle reveals the fail-ures of the politics of respectability and the severe damage it caused to her relationship with Noah. The politics of respectability is often framed and taught to women as the desirable goal because it should serve as a protective space. By covering up their bodies in public, Black church women are able to resist racial and sexual exploitation.[46] Instead, the power dynamics of her family and church dynamics caused Grace to flee from her situation and her relationship with Noah.

The fear of her uncle, Mac, and her silencing around his advances also manifest in her relationship with Darius, a reporter who is not a member of Calvary. An episode aptly titled "Silence and Loneliness," in season two, reveals the long-term and often little discussed effects of patriarchy and power structures within it that can be incredibly hurtful to women. Although Grace escaped Mac's sexual abuse, this family situation caused her great harm, which continues to negatively affect her romantic relationships. When Darius questions her difficulty opening up to people, Grace reveals that Mac attempted to abuse her a few years before he abused her sister, Faith. Darius replies, "I'm sorry. Th-That's awful." Grace responds, "No, what's awful is that I never told. No one knows but you." As Grace and Darius' conversation continues, Darius tells her, "Grace, look . . . from what you've told me, they didn't believe you when you told them about Faith. They might not have believed you then, either." In this scene, Grace tells Darius why she feels guilty: that's not the point. The point is that I didn't say anything. I spent this whole year asking women to come forward and say what Mac did to them. I never came clean about what happened to me. And now that Mac is dead, it's hitting me harder than ever, the role that I had played in all of this. If I had just said it to Faith, she might still be alive, and I hate that. I hate it, and I can't go back and fix it. I can just move forward. And I don't know how to do that.[47]

Grace's declaration shows her internalizing the consequences of Mac's abuse and her feelings of guilt in a difficult situation, even though she had little power to change or combat it, especially in her youth. Her situation reveals a troubling dynamic for young Black women who are living in seemingly "safe spaces" of churches and traditional, nuclear family structures. This furthers Collins' discussion of questioning assumptions of safety for Black women embedded within social institutions African Americans often utilize to combat systemic racism.[48] In her youth and young adulthood, Grace intertwined church and spirituality—when she left one, she left the other without much examination. Her return symbolizes trying to reintegrate both in her life. This further creates a cycle that continues to perpetuate, as Grace has difficulties navigating silence and agency.

The cycle of silence continues in later seasons, when it is revealed that she and Noah have a son, AJ. Grace put him up for adoption when she was eighteen and never told Noah she was pregnant or that he was the father of their child. When AJ contacts Grace after he has legally become an adult, she learns that although she was attempting to give him a better life, he grew up in a difficult situation and has been incarcerated. Grace perceives this as a wrong that must be corrected but has difficulty resolving this with her role as a pastor. She experiences a spiritual and moral dilemma as she decides how to assist her son. She offers financial assistance but does not want him to be part of her life at Calvary or the Greenleaf family. Her values are put to the test when AJ asks her to be an alibi for a crime he's been accused of committing. Grace decides to lie for him, although she's not sure if that's the right thing to do. She at first attempts to keep him a secret from her family but ultimately decides to tell them. When season four concludes, she unexpectedly decides to resign from her position and decides to stand with AJ. Grace decides to leave her position for her son, reflecting her perception that the Black church will not be understanding or accepting of her current situation.

CONCLUSION

The analysis of Grace Greenleaf's character, particularly in her role as associate pastor and activist, reflects the nuances of contemporary women leaders in Black churches. Although a fictional drama, some fans perceive the character portrayals and storylines of the show as "real life,"[49] showcasing how *Greenleaf* resonates with viewers. Grace's character reflects tensions between women's empowerment and social justice with traditionally gendered church dynamics. It extends Alice Walker's notion of women being in love and in trouble with relationships that engage churches and spirituality, bringing together two aspects of womanist thought. Furthermore, Grace's character analysis reflects ways that womanist tenets work in tandem with aspects of Black feminist thought, particularly as they connect to the notion of "safe spaces." Grace exemplifies how advocating for women, and other matters of social justice, can take place both within Black churches and in secular spaces.

Although this chapter focused primarily on her role as an associate pastor, future studies could examine the tension between secular and spiritual identities. This would deepen the connection between being in love and in trouble for women with more social power and prominent roles in the church. It would also be interesting to examine the familial dynamics Grace experiences with her immediate family members, particularly the relationships she has with her parents. Bishop Greenleaf functions as a safe space for Grace to create and expand avenues for women's advocacy, although she moves in secrecy from him at times. Her relationship with her mother, Lady Mae Greenleaf, however, is much more problematic and contentious. Grace Greenleaf's character reflects both positive, uplifting attributes of women leaders in Black churches and more constraining ones. Although there has been much progress regarding the role of women in Black churches, this character portrayal sheds light on the work that still needs to be done to advance women in religious and spiritual spaces.

NOTES

1. *Greenleaf*, Season 1 episode 4, "Behind Closed Doors," Directed by Clement Virgo Aired June 29, 2016, OWN Network, https://www.netflix.com/watch/80141070.

2. Carmen B. Williams and Marsha I. Wiggins, "Womanist Spirituality as a Response to the Racism-Sexism Double Bind in African American Women," *Counseling & Values*, no. 2 (2010): 175–186. https://doi-org.libproxy.uncg.edu/10.1002/j.2161-007X.2010.tb00015.x.

3. Alice Walker, *In Search of Our Mothers' Gardens: Womanist Prose* (San Diego: Harcourt Brace Jovanovich, 1983).

4. Walker, *In Search of Our Mothers' Gardens*; Patricia H. Collins, *Black Feminist Thought: Knowledge, Consciousness, and the Politics of Empowerment* (New York: Routledge, 2000); Williams and Wiggins, "Womanist Spirituality."

5. Walker, *In Search of Our Mothers' Gardens*.

6. Collins, *Black Feminist Thought*.

7. Collins, *Black Feminist Thought*.

8. Sandra M. Schneiders, "Feminist Spirituality," in *The New Dictionary of Catholic Spirituality*, ed. Michael Downey (Collegeville: Liturgical Press, 1993), 395.

9. Andrew Billingsley and Cleopatra H. Caldwell. "The Church, the Family, and the School in the African American Community," *The Journal of Negro Education*, no. 3 (1991): 427–440. doi: 10.2307/2295494.

10. Kimberly P. Johnson, *The Womanist Preacher: Proclaiming Womanist Rhetoric from the Pulpit* (Lanham, MD: Lexington Books, 2017).

11. Collins, *Black Feminist Thought*; Alice Walker, *In Love & Trouble: Stories of Black Women* (New York: Houghton Mifflin Harcourt, 2004).

12. Katie G. Canon, *Katie's Canon: Womanism and the Soul of the Black Community* (New York, NY: Continuum, 1995).

13. Julia A.J. Foote, "Women in the Gospel," in *Words of Fire: An Anthology of African-American Feminist Thought*, eds. Beverly Guy-Sheftall (New York, NY: The New Press, 1995), 52–53.

14. Melanie C. Jones, "The Will to Adorn: Beyond Self-Surveillance, toward a Womanist Ethic of Redemptive Self-Love," *Black Theology: An International Journal*, no. 3 (2018): 218–230. https://doi-org.libproxy.uncg.edu/10.1080/14769948.2018.1492303.

15. Jones, "The Will to Adorn."

16. Collins, *Black Feminist Thought*.

17. Walker, *In Love & Trouble*.

18. Collins, *Black Feminist Thought.*

19. Collins, *Black Feminist Thought*; Alice Walker, *In Love & Trouble: Stories of Black Women* (New York: Houghton Mifflin Harcourt, 2004).

20. Terrie M. Williams, *Black Pain: It Just Looks Like We're Not Hurting* (New York: Scribner, 2008).

21. Janette Y. Taylor, "No Resting Place: African American Women at the Crossroads of Violence," *Violence against Women*, no. 11 (2005): 1473–1489. https ://doi.org/10.1177/1077801205280275.

22. Patricia H. Collins, *Black Sexual Politics: African Americans, Gender and the New Racism* (New York: Routledge, 2004).

23. Cerise L. Glenn and Andrew R. Spieldenner, "An Intersectional Analysis"; Collins, *Black Feminist Thought*; Walker, *In Love & Trouble.*

24. Cassandra Chaney, "Who Is David and Who Is Goliath? The Eddie Long Scandal and the Black Mega-Church," *Mental Health, Religion & Culture*, no. 1 (2013): 58–78. https://doi.org/10.1080/13674676.2011.645224.

25. Joshua Atkinson and Calafell M. Bernadette, "Darth Vader Made Me Do It!: Anakin Skywalker's Avoidance of Responsibility and the Gray Areas of Hegemonic Masculinity in the Star Wars Universe," *Communication, Culture Critique* 2, no. 1 (2009): 1–20. https://doi.org/10.1111/j.1753-9137.2008.01026.x.

26. Khalia J. Williams, "Engaging Womanist Spirituality in African American Christian Worship," *Proceedings of the North American Academy of Liturgy* (2013): 95–109.

27. *Greenleaf*, Season 1 episode 9, "One Train May Hide Another," Directed by Clement Virgo Aired July 20, 2016, OWN Network, https://www.netflix.com/watch /80141075.

28. Evelyn B. Higginbotham, *The Politics of Respectability. In Righteous Discontent: The Women's Movement in the Black Baptist Church* (Cambridge, MA: Harvard University Press, 1993).

29. Allissa V. Richardson, "Dismantling Respectability: The Rise of New Womanist Communication Models in the Era of Black Lives Matter," *Journal of Communication*, no. 2 (2019): 193–213. https://doi.org/10.1093/joc/jqz005.

30. Margot Adeler, "Before Rosa Parks, There Was Claudette Colvin," NPR, March 15, 2009; Phillip Hoose, *Claudette Colvin: Twice Toward Justice* (New York: Melanie Kroupa Books, 2009).

31. Monique Moultrie, "Putting a Ring on It: Black Women, Black Churches, and Coerced Monogamy," *Black Theology: An International Journal*, no. 3 (2018): 231–247. https://doi.org/10.1080/14769948.2018.1492304.

32. *Greenleaf*, Season 3 episode 8, "Dea Abscondita," Directed by Clement Virgo. Aired October 17, 2018, OWN Network, https://www.netflix.com/watch/80988321.

33. Mary A. Bock and Ever Josue Figueroa. "Faith and Reason: An Analysis of the Homologies of Black and Blue Lives Facebook Pages," *New Media and Society*, no. 9 (2018): 3097–3118. https://doi.org/10.1177/1461444817740822; Amanda N. Edgar and Andre E. Johnson, *The Struggle over Black Lives Matter and All Lives Matter.* Rhetoric, Race, and Religion (Lanham, MD: Lexington Books 2018).

34. Hect, Jackson, and Ribeau, *African American Communication.*

35. Jones, "The Will to Adorn."

36. *Greenleaf*, Season 1 episode 4, "Behind Closed Doors," Directed by Clement Virgo Aired June 29, 2016, OWN Network, https://www.netflix.com/watch/80141070.

37. Billingsley and Caldwell, "The Church."

38. Bock and Figueroa, "Faith and Reason."

39. Leah G. Francis, *Ferguson &Faith: Sparking Leadership & Awakening Community* (St. Louis, MO: Chalice Press, 2015).

40. *Greenleaf*, "Behind Closed Doors."

41. Cerise L. Glenn and Dante L. Johnson, ""What They See as Acceptable": A Co-Cultural Theoretical Analysis of Black Male Students at a Predominantly White Institution," *Howard Journal of Communications*, no. 4 (2012): 351–368. https://doi.org/10.1080/10646175.2012.722817.

42. Moultrie, "Putting a Ring on It."

43. Walker, *In Love & Trouble;* Collins, *Black Feminist Thought.*

44. *Greenleaf*, Season 1 episode 8, "The Whole Book," Directed by Clement Virgo Aired July 27, 2016, OWN Network, https://www.netflix.com/watch/80141074.

45. Chaney, "Who Is David."

46. Jones, "The Will to Adorn."

47. *Greenleaf*, Season 2 episode 13, "Silence and Loneliness," Directed by Clement Virgo Aired September 6, 2017, OWN Network, https://www.netflix.com/watch/80185219.

48. Collins, *Black Feminist Thought.*

49. Joyce Dixon, Comment on Google Reviews, January 23, 2020.

BIBLIOGRAPHY

Adler, M. 2009. "Before Rosa Parks, There Was Claudette Colvin. Minnesota Public Radio." NPR. April 3, 2020, Available from: https://www.npr.org/2009/03/15/101719889/before-rosa-parks-there-was-claudette-colvin.

Atkinson, Joshua, and Bernadette M. Calafell. 2009. "Darth Vader Made Me Do It!: Anakin Skywalker's Avoidance of Responsibility and the Gray Areas of Hegemonic Masculinity in the Star Wars Universe." *Communication, Culture & Critique* 2, no. 1, 1–20. doi: 10.1111/j.1753-9137.2008.01026.x.

Billingsley, Andrew and Cleopatra H. Caldwell. 1991. The Church, the Family, and the School in the African American Community. *The Journal of Negro Education*, no. 3, 427–440. doi: 10.2307/2295494.

Bock, Mary A., and Ever Josue Figueroa. 2018. "Faith and Reason: An Analysis of the Homologies of Black and Blue Lives Facebook Pages." *New Media and Society,* no. 9 (November), 3097–3118. doi: 10.1177/1461444817740822.

Canon, Katie G. 1995. *Katie's Canon: Womanism and the Soul of the Black Community. Community.* United Kingdom: Continuum.

Chaney, Cassandra. 2013. "Who Is David and Who Is Goliath? The Eddie Long Scandal and the Black Mega-Church." *Mental Health, Religion & Culture*, no. 1 (February), 58–78. doi: 10.1080/13674676.2011.645224.

Collins, Patricia H. 2000. *Black Feminist Thought : Knowledge, Consciousness, and the Politics of Empowerment.* Routledge Classics. New York: Routledge.

Collins, Patricia. H. 2004. *Black Sexual Politics: African Americans, Gender and the New Racism.* New York, NY: Routledge.

Dixon, Joyce, January 23, 2020, Comment on Google Reviews.

Edgar, Amanda N., and Andre E. Johnson. 2018. *The Struggle over Black Lives Matter and All Lives Matter.* Rhetoric, Race, and Religion. Lanham, MD: Lexington Books, an imprint of The Rowman & Littlefield Publishing Group.

Foote, Julia A. J. 1995. Women in the Gospel. In *Words of fire: An Anthology of African-American Feminist Thought*, edited by Beverly Guy-Sheftall, 52–53. New York, NY: The New Press.

Francis, Leah G. 2015. *Ferguson & Faith: Sparking Leadership & Awakening Community*, First ed. St. Louis, MO: Chalice Press.

Glenn, Cerise L., and Andrew R. Spieldenner. 2013. "An Intersectional Analysis of Television Narratives of African American Women with African American Men on 'the Down Low.'" *Sexuality & Culture*, no. 3, 401–416. https://doi.org/10.1007/s12119-013-9189-y.

Glenn, Cerise L., and Dante L. Johnson. 2012. "What They See as Acceptable:" A Co-Cultural Theoretical Analysis of Black Male Students at a Predominantly White Institution." *Howard Journal of Communications*, no. 4, 351–368. doi: 10.1080/10646175.2012.722817.

Hecht, Michael L., Jackson II, Ronald L., and Sidney A. Ribeau. 2003. *African American Communication: Exploring Identity and Culture.* Mahwah, NJ: Lawrence Erlbaum Associates, Inc.

Higginbotham, Evelyn B. 1993. *The Politics of Respectability. In Righteous Discontent: The Women's Movement in the Black Baptist Church.* Cambridge, MA: Harvard University Press.

Hoose, Phillip. 2009. *Claudette Colvin: Twice Toward Justice.* New York: Melanie Kroupa Books.

Johnson, Kimberly P. 2017. *The Womanist Preacher: Proclaiming Womanist Rhetoric from the Pulpit.* Lexington Books.

Jones, Melanie C. 2018. The Will to Adorn: Beyond Self-Surveillance, toward a Womanist Ethic of Redemptive Self-Love. *Black Theology: An International Journal*, no. 3, 218–230. doi: 10.1080/14769948.2018.1492303.

Moultrie, Monique. 2018. Putting a Ring on It: Black Women, Black Churches, and Coerced Monogamy. *Black Theology: An International Journal*, no. 3, 231–247. doi: 10.1080/14769948.2018.1492304.

Richardson, Allissa V. 2019. Dismantling Respectability: The Rise of New Womanist Communication Models in the Era of Black Lives Matter. *Journal of Communication*, no. 2 (March), 193–213. doi: 10.1093/joc/jqz005.

Sandra M. Schneiders. 1993. "Feminist Spirituality." In *The New Dictionary of Catholic Spirituality*, edited by Michael Downey, no. 69, 395. Collegeville: Liturgical Press.

Taylor, Janette Y. 2005. "No Resting Place: African American Women at the Crossroads of Violence." *Violence against Women* 11, no. 12, 1473–1489. doi: 10.1177/1077801205280275.

Walker, Alice. 2004. *In Love & Trouble: Stories of Black Women.* New York: Houghton Mifflin Harcourt.

Walker, Alice. 1983. *In Search of Our Mothers' Gardens : Womanist Prose.* San Diego: Harcourt Brace Jovanovich.

Williams, Khalia J. 2013. Engaging Womanist Spirituality in African American Christian Worship. *Proceedings of the North American Academy of Liturgy,* (August), 95–109.

Williams, Terrie M. 2008. *Black Pain: It Just Looks Like We're Not Hurting.* New York: Scribner.

Williams, Carmen B and Marsha I. Wiggins. 2010. Womanist Spirituality as a Response to the Racism-Sexism Double Bind in African American Women. *Counseling & Values,* no. 2, 175–186. doi: 10.1002/j.2161-007X.2010.tb00015.x.

Wright, Craig, writer. *Greenleaf.* Season 1 episode 4, "Behind Closed Doors." Directed by Clement Virgo. Aired June 29, 2016b, on OWN Network, https://www .netflix.com/watch/80141070.

Wright, Craig, writer. Greenleaf. Season 1 episode 8, "The Whole Book." Directed by Clement Virgo. Aired July 27, 2016c, on OWN Network, https://www.netflix .com/watch/80141074.

Wright, Craig, writer. *Greenleaf.* Season 1 episode 9, "One Train May Hide Another." Directed by Clement Virgo. Aired July 20, 2016d, on OWN Network, https://www .netflix.com/watch/80141075.

Wright, Craig, writer. *Greenleaf.* Season 2 episode 13, "Silence and Loneliness." Directed by Clement Virgo. Aired September 6, 2017, on OWN Network, https:// www.netflix.com/watch/80185219.

Wright, Craig, writer. *Greenleaf.* Season 3 episode 8, "Dea Abscondita." Directed by Clement Virgo. Aired October 17, 2018, on OWN Network, https://www.netflix .com/watch/80988321.

Chapter 4

"The Beloved Language Community"

A Call for Womanism and Language to Address the Racial Academic Achievement Gap

Kami J. Anderson

In preparing this chapter, there are two quotes that can be recalled that bring to focus the need to have discourse around the beloved community and the foreign language classroom. Anya notes, "African American lives are powerfully mediated by race and fundamentally shaped by racialized consciousness and identities . . . experiences in learning a new language are no exception to that."[1] Couple this with Thurman's charge to "meet people where they are, but deal with them as though they are where they should be"[2] and you find the foundation for our discussion concerning social justice and the foreign language classroom. "Social justice" has become the buzz phrase slowly replacing "multicultural education" in the K–12 classroom. This is a controversial start to a chapter in a book about womanist ideology and social justice; however, let us unpack the intent behind the statement. From the perspective of a preservice teacher, those students who are still training for the education degree, social justice has been described as an examination of how "positionality biases their epistemology."[3] The charge is preservice teachers should adopt reflective practices prior to leaving the university in order to lessen the possibility of being culturally mismatched in their classrooms. The historic stance of multicultural education was to address the need for teachers to be "prepared with the knowledge, skills, and dispositions to work effectively with students and communities whose cultural perspective and lived experiences differ from their own."[4] The intention was to address the gap in intercultural awareness between newly serviced teachers and the students they serve.

The unintended consequence further marginalizes the teacher from the student in the classroom. Diverse perspectives are not fully valued in the classroom, and instead, what emerges are growing disparities in educational opportunity and achievement.[5] Anya argues, "Despite our best intentions and aspirations toward positive values of color blindness, black students are acutely aware of and impacted by the messages communicated through the exclusion of these critical considerations."[6] This charge implies distinct assumptions that stand in contradiction to the true meaning of social justice and, by association, community in the classroom. In fact, it can be argued that true social justice in the classroom embodies the characteristics of womanist pedagogy. Picower offers six elements of social justice in the classroom:

1. Have self-love and knowledge.
2. Gain respect for the history and characteristics of people different from themselves.
3. Critically examine how identities impact peoples' lived and material conditions.
4. Teach how people fought against oppression through social movements.
5. Engage in activities that increase awareness of others in their community around social issues.[7]
6. Experience what it means to struggle for justice through social action.

These six elements draw on similarities to womanist pedagogy and the cocreation of community. As Cannon, Gise Johnson, and Sims put forth, "African American women know that in pursuit of knowledge we need time to explore a complex of discouraging realities."[8] They further assert that "there is a burning desire to excavate the pragmatic survivalist intentions and relational convictions that enable people of African descent to connect worldwide as members of the African diaspora."[9] These scholars charge that womanist pedagogy should and does engage the convergence of academic success, civic engagement, and community activism through the classroom and course content.

In this chapter, I seek to discuss the importance of centric pedagogy. I argue for the focus of womanist pedagogy when it comes to effectively teaching the Black[10] child in one classroom in particular—the foreign language classroom. Both of these can have a significant impact on how students can not only learn foreign languages but *retain* them long term. The insertion of these pedagogies can drive the foreign language classroom to cocreate the beloved community with Black students in order to foster a sense of belonging, which will further success in the course.

This is a social justice issue in that the academic success of marginalized groups is part and parcel of radical resistance to the oppressive heteronormative system of education in the United States. This chapter will introduce the concept of liberatory bilingualism as a womanist methodology for ensuring academic success while simultaneously cocreating a beloved community through language by black students in the foreign language classroom.

Using critical language and race theory[11] as a lens, this chapter will begin with discussing the current concerns in the foreign language classroom by explaining cultural mismatch theory. Crump[12] explains critical language and race theory (LangCrit), as the point of intersection and negotiation of linguistic and racialized identities in multilingual spaces. It is important to note that LangCrit is a bit different from critical language theory in that it centers race and linguistics at their intersection and with intentionality. I will then move to discussing the need for culturally relevant pedagogy and how womanist pedagogy qualifies as such. Finally, I will address ways to infuse and implement womanist pedagogical practices and strategies for the foreign language classroom.

LIBERATORY BILINGUALISM

Akkari argues that "language is a political instrument in that it provides a means and proof of power."[13] By definition, liberatory bilingualism "includes using the power of mastering several languages and/or dialects to seek cultural, social, economic, and political equality with the dominant group."[14] Although this definition was intended for students with English as a second language, when arguing for social justice for students of color in the foreign language classroom, this same definition can be used as a pedagogical tool for allowing students of color, Black students, in particular, to generate their power and knowledge through language learning. Liberatory bilingualism answers the charge of Westfield for womanist pedagogy to have "an unwavering agenda of liberation"[15] and the call from Cannon, Gise Johnson, and Sims that "black womanist liberationists do not fit neatly in top traditional departments and disciplines."[16] Liberatory bilingualism challenges current foreign language learning pedagogy. It demonstrates my willingness as a womanist scholar to "raise new questions in our various disciplines of study by generating knowledge pertinent to black women's angle of vision."[17]

In order to properly address social justice in the foreign language classroom, we must first acknowledge the presence of the Black student in the classroom and, second, allow them agency and empowerment through language while there. This will offer a move toward liberatory education in the foreign language classroom. The introduction of pedagogical practices such as hip hop pedagogy,[18] Afrocentric pedagogy,[19] and womanist pedagogy[20] that center the Black child has proven effective in other content areas, but the practices have yet to be applied in the foreign classroom.

Let's be clear: this is *not* new. In fact, for more than 100 years, starting with Dr. Anna Julia Cooper and Dr. W. E. B. Du Bois,[21] there has been constant and consistent discourse about what would help Black students thrive and achieve to their highest potential. The information you will find in this chapter is compiled and repurposed, gathered to fit the argument for foreign language learning and the Black student. It is not innovative. It is not brand new. It is a megaphone being added to a conversation that has been persistently muted when it comes to academic achievement for the Black child.

When discussing pedagogy for the Black child, there has been some attention given to centering the historical experiences of African Americans through Afrocentric and womanist pedagogy.[22] The research has been relegated to African American scholars with little inclusion and integration into the overall conversations of teaching and learning. The lack of language-centered pedagogical inclusion has done the African American in education, both teacher and student, a disservice. When examining womanist pedagogy as a form of liberatory education, one must understand how this pedagogy "can liberate students who are often disadvantaged by race, class, gender, and age; then one must consider the efficacy of this pedagogy as a means to empower others who experience oppression."[23] The foreign language classroom is often overlooked as a space in need of a critical race lens because the content area boasts "culture" as one of the primary goals of the discipline. The American Council for Teachers of Foreign Languages[24] stipulates that the five "C" goal areas—communication, cultures, connections, comparisons, and communities—are to "prepare learners to apply the skills and understandings measured by the Standards, to bring global competence to their future career and experiences."[25] More specifically, the goal area of culture, defined as "interact with cultural competence and understanding,"[26] is achieved as "learners use language to investigate, explain, and reflect on the relationship between the practices, products, and perspectives of the cultures studied."[27]

However, Anya[28] points out rather plainly, "African Americans have been excluded from meaningful participation in foreign language education."[29] How can a content area that purports cultural competence as a goal not consider the impact of current pedagogical practices through critical language and race theory[30] in order to develop cultural awareness and competence in students of color? To answer this question, one must address cultural incongruencies between teachers and students of color in the foreign language classroom.

CULTURALLY MISMATCHED

The concept of being "culturally mismatched" seems self-explanatory, but in efforts to make sure that it is not glossed over or dismissed as nonconsequential to the teaching process, it is important to offer perspective. The theory, initially asserted by Lessow Hurley,[31] suggests that when the teacher and student are not able to come together relationally because their lived experiences are so far removed from one another, it can impede learning in the classroom. What does this look like? Something as simple as the sad look you give the student who has worn the same shirt to school for the past three days, without acknowledging that said shirt is clean and neatly pressed every day. It is not paying attention to the mischievousness and bullying present among the girls because you are more fixated on the antics of the boys and assume they will be the most disruptive. It is shaking your head at the Black girls twerk dancing in the cafeteria and chalking it up as being oversexualized and thereby questioning their reports of harassment and sexual abuse in school or at home. The negative perceptions of these outward displays of culture can cause a teacher who may not adopt Afrocentric or womanist pedagogy to impose consequences for their presence in the classroom. The womanist teacher would instead acknowledge the tensions between performances of race and gender with students of color and the performance of whiteness and gender by educators.[32] Recognizing and acknowledging this tension would then allow the teacher to use "cultural knowledge, learning styles, lived experiences of students and strengths of students to establish meaningful connections between the students socio-cultural realities and the academic experiences in the classroom."[33]

In the foreign language classroom, the practices imposed on students of color are oppressive in that they impede success in the classroom. The absence of African descendants in Spanish language culture and history, the assumption that students of color enter the foreign language classroom already at a deficit due to perceived inadequacies in the English language,[34] and under-representation of Black foreign language teachers are poignant examples of the need to introduce liberatory practices in the foreign language classroom. Reports of racist teacher and peer attitudes, low expectations, and irrelevant learning materials are just a few of the examples noted in research.[35]

We need to call these examples of what they are: microaggressions in the classroom. To alleviate and eliminate these microaggressive behaviors, the practice of introspection would need to be more than a one-semester-long course or reflective essay at the end of Student Teaching Practicums. For non-African American teachers, "it would require a willingness to conduct critical self-examinations about assumptions, beliefs, and stereotypes they may have about African American students. More importantly, how have these assumptions negatively or positively affect the teaching and learning process for such students."[36] In the foreign language classroom, the cultural mismatch is practiced through teaching materials and methodologies that ignore black presence and diminish black voice in the course materials and the classroom.

Cultural mismatch is also the lack of Black foreign language teachers in the classroom. The most recent report of DataUSA on the number of teachers who identify as Black is 3.27% and white teacher represent over 50% of the degrees awarded in foreign language education[37] (2016). In fact African Americans only account for 4% of foreign language degrees regardless of whether they enter into the teaching workforce.[38] These practices are oppressive at best and oblivious to the noteworthy contributions black bodies have within the content area of languages and also in the classroom through the voices and participation of black students.

Womanist pedagogy speaks to the importance of representation. Hardy explains the goal should be to "seek to legitimize the voice and visibility of students."[39] She further purports that womanist pedagogy as a performative act involves practices "that raise student and teacher critical gendered and racial consciousness."[40] As previously argued with the introduction of multicultural education, the absence of cultural understanding falls on the ability of the teacher to see the "well being of the whole child as it is not only concerned with students' academic achievement but also seeks to help students maintain their cultural identity and heritage."[41] One of the methods to employ these practices is using culturally relevant pedagogy.

"Culturally sensitive pedagogy is tied to the belief that if learning structures and stimuli are grounded in a cultural context familiar to students, the potential for cognitive expansion is enhanced."[42] So what does this even mean? It is an argument for centering the experiences of Black children in the learning process. We have seen how Math teachers incorporate music, how ELA/Reading teachers select texts with Black child protagonists, but in the foreign language classroom, this type of relevancy stops at kinesthetic learning, or what foreign language teachers commonly referred to as Total Physical Response.[43] In order for the foreign language classroom to have culturally relevant pedagogy, there must be holistic instruction strategies that ensure that Black students become

1. intellectually capable;
2. socially adaptable;
3. morally sound; and
4. empowered through self-awareness and agency in their own achievement.

These tenets are the foundation of womanist pedagogy.

WOMANISM AND THE FOREIGN
LANGUAGE CLASSROOM

To begin to understand how womanism can be seen as social justice in the classroom, I recall my reference to Dr. Anna Julia Cooper. Sule states that "educated Black women realized that their fate was inextricably tied to the masses . . . [Cooper's] everyday—her blackness and femaleness—served as explicit starting and ending points to her social critiques."[44] Black women engage in activism often in ways that do not explicitly look like resistance. This can be seen in how Black women perform in the classroom. Womanism is a social change perspective rooted in Black women's and other women of color's everyday experiences and everyday methods of problem solving. The crucial component to this theory and ideology is that these methods of problem solving happen in everyday spaces, not merely in the classroom. The focus is to address the problem of ending all forms of oppression for all people, restoring balance between people and the environment/nature, and reconciling human life with the spiritual dimension.

There are three things that womanist scholars understand: (1) oppression is an interlinked system that offers both penalty and privilege simultaneously, (2) empowerment and collective action and agency are what will bring about sustainable transformation, and (3) liberation is for everyone not just Black women. In womanist pedagogy, there is a union of power and caring, spirituality and pedagogy, personal agency and collectivism. One can argue these components, when intentionally addressed, can sustain a beloved language community. What does this look like in the classroom?

First and foremost must be the belief that the students are capable of being academically successful.[45] Once this is established, one can begin the process of liberatory education in the foreign language classroom. Beauboef-Lafontant argues that womanist pedagogy combines power and caring,[46] which she names, "politicized mothering,"[47] drawing on an ethic of risk[48] by choosing to empower Black students despite any obstacles toward social change because "fighting oppression is a way of caring."[49] This means that there are characteristics that are inherent to womanism. Besides being a critical theory that has a social justice lens, womanism as a teaching methodology must also include:

- antioppressionist ideology;
- the use of vernacular;
- be nonideological;
- be communitarian; and
- have a spiritualized component.

Now, these components go against what we understand of the classroom, classroom management, and effective teaching strategies. The Westernized focus of the curriculum, the separation of church and state in the public education system, individualized achievement and learning styles that center and reward the use of Mainstream American English over the vernacular—all contradict the primary characteristics of womanist teaching. Let us examine how the five components can be implemented in the foreign language classroom.

ANTIOPPRESSIONIST IDEOLOGY AND THE USE OF THE VERNACULAR

Anya argues, "Racism goes far beyond overt displays of bigotry."[50] Oppressive practices in the foreign language classroom are the subtle ways difference is silenced and ignored. Even when the Black student is excited about the language classroom, when the practices of a given language-learning environment reinforce elitism, sexism, racism, or homophobia, the student can feel excluded from participation.[51] This feeling of exclusion can manifest as disinterest and the oppressive lens assumes a lack of motivation or poor ability. Potowski calls for the charge for teachers to "link students' classroom language use to the ongoing production of their identities."[52]

This would require the foreign language classroom to acknowledge and incorporate not only anti-oppressionist ideologies but the use of vernacular in both languages in order to demonstrate true investment of Black identity with language use and to acknowledge the womanist concept that "language learning is a complex social practice that engages the identities of language learners in ways that have received little attention."[53] This can be achieved by including practices such as Afrolatino examples of speaking and Afrolatino history and culture as a part of the content. These practices should not be presented as an afterthought but rather embedded in pedagogical content in ways that are seamless and fluid.

BUILDING COMMUNITY

Critical to our understanding of social justice and the classroom is the significant impact modeling the beloved community has with academic success. Mandel argues that "in the beloved community the diverse peoples of the United States, and ultimately the world reconciled their differences, integrated, cooperated, and coexisted with one another."[54] This charges the foreign language classroom, especially to leave no person, ethnic group, or marginalized populations muted or absent from its pedagogy. Mandel further asserts that "public schools particularly have become . . . the act of creating and dispersing knowledge throughout a society."[55] This responsibility requires the classroom to develop the beloved society articulated by King in his speeches and writings. This gives particular care and attention to the Black student in the foreign language classroom by centering their presence not just physically but also within course content and curriculum.

One can establish the "beloved community" espoused by Howard Thurman in liberation theology, by building a collective, shared identity with and among the students in the foreign language classroom. This could be continuing a practice that is already present in many foreign language classrooms but with a greater intention for womanist pedagogy: music. Rankow suggests that "music helps kinesthetic (and other) learners integrate the material by using both hemispheres of the brain."[56] Durham also argues that from a hip hop feminist standpoint, centering popular culture; one can reimagine the dynamic of possibilities of a feminist politics for surviving, escaping, and dismantling colluding exploitive systems. Although Durham's argument is intended specifically for Black girls as collective, the sentiment through a womanist lens can extend to Black boys within the foreign language classroom as well. As a former Spanish teacher in the K–12 classroom, I was able to see how an innocent inclusion of Hip Hop Friday in my Spanish class opened the doors linguistically for my students.[57] This simple practice of including music my students preferred to listen to was a praxical demonstration of how, as a womanist teacher, I see "racism and other systemic injustices as simultaneously social and educational" and use cultural artifacts that address these injustices intentionally as a teaching tool for language in my classroom.

SPIRITUALITY AND SACRED SPACE

The final trait of the womanist classroom, the spiritualized component, is paramount to womanist pedagogy but antithetical to the current public education classroom. It can, however, be incorporated by keeping Thurman's intention of the "beloved community" centered in classroom instruction and classroom management. This is achieved by maintaining a "disciplines employment of love as a force for personal and social transformation."[58] This goes beyond womanist strategies such as "other mothering"[59] but expands to include "spirituality as an integral part of human existence"[60] that seeks to humanize people through education. Hardy argues that by embracing spirituality within womanist pedagogy, it "conceives motherhood more broadly as a womanist method for social transformation."[61]

CONCLUSION

Multicultural education is not an old concept. It took twenty years *after Brown v Board of Education* in Topeka, Kansas, for educators to realize they were not fully equipped to teach a culturally diverse classroom. I was born twenty years after *Brown v Board of Education*. If multicultural education were a person, it would be a GenXer. Let that sink in for a moment. This chapter provides a starting point for the reimagining of how education can be used for building the beloved language community. I have many people in my age group who are finding themselves, reinventing themselves, reimagining their life moving forward. Metaphorically speaking, multicultural education assesses and evaluates itself similarly for the sake of its sustainability and generational wealth. Although the intention was to address the gap in intercultural awareness between newly serviced teachers and the students they serve, the unintended consequence further marginalizes the teacher from the student in the classroom. Diverse perspectives are not fully valued in the classroom, and instead, what emerges are growing disparities in educational opportunity and achievement.

By adopting womanist pedagogy, particularly in the foreign language classroom, teachers are able to engage both the intellectual and embodied knowledge of their students. The maternal image that comes with womanist ideologies combines power and caring in the foreign language classroom to empower students through images and careful curation of cultural legacy to make language a political tool of liberation and academic achievement for the Black child. This focus would create a beloved language community for the success of the Black child in the foreign language classroom.

NOTES

1. See Anya, 2018.
2. See Thurman, 1976.
3. See Takacs, 2000, p. 170.
4. McAllister & Irvine as cited in Cherng & Davis, 2019, p. 219.
5. See Cherng and Davis, 2019.
6. Anya, 2018, p. 217.
7. See Picower, 2005.
8. See Cannon, Gise Johnson and Sims, 2005, p. 135.
9. Ibid, pp. 137–138.
10. I use the term "Black" in order to encompass students who identify as being of African descent living in the United States regardless of connection to the period of enslavement within the country. While I am clear that scholars operationalize the distinctions between African American and Black in different ways, my scholarly definition of Black is intentionally broad.
11. See Anya, 2018.

12. See Crump 2014.

13. Akkari, 1998, p. 115.

14. Ibid., p. 115.

15. See Westfield, 2003, p. 522.

16. Op cit., p. 135.

17. Ibid, p. 143.

18. See Durham 2014; Love, 2018.

19. See Asante 1998; Watkins, 2006.

20. See Beauboeuf-Lafontant, 2002; Hardy 2009.

21. See Alridge, 2007.

22. See Howard, 2001; Beauboeuf-Lafontant, 2002; Westfield, 2003; Watkins, 2006: Hardy, 2009.

23. Hardy, 2009, p. 57.

24. Also written as ACTFL.

25. http://actfl.org retrieved September 8, 2019.

26. Ibid.

27. http://actfl.org retrieved September 13, 2019.

28. See Anya, 2018.

29. Ibid, p. 5.

30. Ibid, np.

31. See Lessow Hurley, 1986.

32. See Hardy, 2009.

33. Ibid, p. 25.

34. See Bereiter & Englemann, 1966; Deutsch, 1967.

35. See Davis, 1992; Glyn, 2012; Anya, 2018.

36. Howard, 2001, p. 199.

37. DataUSA, 2016.

38. See Anya, 2018.

39. Hardy, 2009, p. 27.

40. Ibid, p. 42.

41. Hardy, 2009, p. 25.

42. Howard, 2001, p. 182.

43. Also referred to as TPR in foreign language pedagogical practices.

44. See Sule, 2014.

45. See Howard, 2001.

46. See Beaubeof-Lafontant, 2002.

47. Ibid, 1999.

48. See Hardy, 2009.

49. Ibid, p. 39.

50. Anya, 2018, p. 42.

51. Ibid.

52. Potowski, 2007, p. 93.

53. Ibid, p. 3.

54. Mandel, 2006, pp. 3–4.

55. Ibid, p. 4.

56. Rankow, 2008, pp. 198–199.

57. I was a Spanish 1, 2, and 3 teacher in both middle school and high school from 2002 to 2005.
58. Rankow, 2008, p. 202.
59. See Beauboeuf-Lafontant, 2002.
60. Hardy, 2009, p. 37.
61. Ibid, p. 38.

BIBLIOGRAPHY

Akkari, A. (1998). Bilingual Education: Beyond Linguistic Instrumentalization. *Bilingual Research Journal* 22, 103–125.

Aldridge, D. (2007). Of Victorianism, Civilization Is and Progressivism: The Educational Ideas of Anna Julia Cooper and WEB DuBois 1892–1940. *History of Education Quarterly* 47, 416–446.

Anya, U. (2018). *Racialized Identities in Second Language Learning: Speaking Blackness in Brazil*. New York: Routledge.

Beauboeuf-Lafontant, T. (2002). A Womanist Experience of Caring: Understanding the Pedagogy of Exemplary Black Women Teachers. *The Urban Review*, 34, 71–86.

Cannon, K.G., Gise Johnson, A.P., and Sims, A.D. (2005). Living It Out: Womanist Works in the Word. *Journal of Feminist Studies in Religion*, 21, 135–146.

Collins P.H. (2000). "Black Feminist Epistemology." in *Black Feminist Thought*. New York: Routledge. https://datausa.io/profile/cip/foreign-language-teacher-education#demographics (retrieved September 20, 2019).

Hardy, K. (2009). *Womanist Performative Pedagogy*. Chapel Hill: University of North Carolina.

Howard, T. C. (2001) Powerful Pedagogy for African American Students: A Case of Four Teachers. *Urban Education*, 36 (2), 179–202.

Mandel, J. (2006). The Production of a Beloved Community: *Sesame Street*'s Answer to America's Inequalities. *Journal of American Culture*, 29, 3–13.

Picower, B. (2012). Using Their Words: Six Elements of Social Justice Curriculum Design for the Elementary Classroom. *International Journal of Multicultural Education*, 14, 1–17.

Potowski, K. (2007). *Language and Identity in a Dual Immersion Classroom*. Clevedon, UK: Multilingual Matters Ltd.

Sule, T. (2014). Intellectual Activism: The Praxis of Dr. Anna Julia Cooper as a Blueprint for Equity-Based Pedagogy. *Feminist Teacher* 23, 211–229.

Takacs, D. (2002). Positionality, Epistemology and Social Justice in the Classroom. *Social Justice* 29, 168–181.

Watkins, A. (2006). The Pedagogy of African American Parents: Learning from Educational Excellence in the African American Community. *Current Issues in Education*, 9, 1–16.

Westfield, N. L. (2003). Toward a Womanist Approach to Pedagogy. *Religious Education* 98, 521–534.

Chapter 5

Is There Room for the Ratchet in the Beloved Community?

If You're Not Liberating Everyone, Are You Really Talking about Freedom?

Michelle Meggs

Martin Luther King Jr.'s Beloved Community offers a global vision of a revolutionary love of humanity, where people have access to and share in the wealth of the earth. The Beloved Community embraces social and economic justice for all and refuses to give credence to the suffering of humanity. In other words, King envisioned a world that embraced agape love and eschewed the myriad of ways the larger culture seeks to divide itself in an unseemly race of one-upmanship. However, when particular groups are asked to sacrifice their privilege and access, they become insular to protect what they believe is theirs, and theirs alone.

Black women, some of whom may not be considered respectable and worthy of inclusion into the Beloved Community, are often shamed and shunned because they do not fit the template of acceptable Black womanhood. As Bettina Love argues, Black women are shamed for being single mothers, their economic status, their sexual choices, and for acting on their desires.[1] The radical idea of, and commitment to, inclusion is challenged when those who are different from what is considered ideal show up and complicate our understanding of radical inclusion. When the proverbial wagons are circled to maintain the status quo, oftentimes, it is Black women who are forced to determine how they will cultivate strategies for self and social transformation.[2] These strategies have produced survival methodologies that resist the daily systemic injustices Black women endure. One of these methodologies is ratchet womanism.

RATCHET WOMANISM

Ratchet womanism is a methodology that eliminates the binary of a good/bad Black womanhood. It is for the "round the way" women and girls who twerk and teach, preach and pole dance, wear bamboo earrings and Burberry suits, and they embody ratchet womanism. As a methodology, ratchet womanism is a form of content analysis that aids in extracting meaning from images, language, and behavior that extends beyond the surface. Ratchet womanism helps understand the subjectivities that often view Black women as deviant and shun them; it acknowledges how Black women speak themselves into existence. It reexamines the actions of Black women like letting loose and enjoying life, using profanity, and speaking truth to power in ways that have often led to them being perceived as angry and, therefore, less than credible.

Ratchet womanism is not limited to women of any particular socioeconomic status because its liberatory edges encompass the experiences of all Black women. As a methodology, ratchet womanism calls for a deeper analysis of the images and actions of Black women to see how they reflect, communicate, and even shape culture. It is a power move to recenter Black women and honor them. It helps uncover the underlying narratives beneath the images of Black women who are often presented as undesirable, and ratchet womanism recognizes the actions that everyday women take to challenge oppression. It affirms that Black women can behave as they please; however, their actions must point toward liberation. Ratchet womanism understands that it is important to recognize how civility, decorum, and manners are used to uphold authority—patriarchy, whiteness, and other forms of privilege—that we are urged to acquiesce to maintaining power dynamics.[3] Ratchet womanism illuminates what the casual viewer may overlook; it seeks out the liberative edges of Black womanhood.

This reconceptualization of ratchet womanism positions Black women uniquely in relation to power and privilege because it places power in the hands of folks at the margins. When Black women employ ratchet womanism, they become too much; they are uncontrollable, dangerous. Their actions become a master class in how to dismantle respectability and reject the shaming from asserting agency over your body. Ratchet womanism provides additional insight into how Black women use their practices and the languages available to them as essential forms of agency to assert identity and build community. When Lizzo literally showed her bare behind during a basketball game, the entire world went crazy.[4] The respectability police, on all platforms, went into overdrive and dragged her for twerking in a thong at a Lakers game. It wasn't so much that she twerked; it was that she had the nerve to show her plus size behind on camera without shame. She was called many names, including attention seeking, fat, and inappropriate.

A ratchet womanism lens reinterprets Lizzo's actions and recognizes that she is communicating something different. It helps to dismiss the binaries that divide Black women. There are no positive or negative images, just realistic ones. There is a tightrope that Black women are forced to walk, and Lizzo refused to do it. Externally, people questioned why she would show her body in a way that makes Black women look bad. Fat, Black girls should cover themselves up and hide. Internally, many people were proud of her and applauded how she loved her body.

Lizzo unapologetically embraces the fullness of who she is. She rejects the politics of shame that surrounds larger bodies, and in particular, larger Black women's bodies. Mocking larger Black bodies is not new, and Lizzo rejects the idea that thinner bodies are more acceptable. There are underlying assumptions that these bodies are unattractive, asexual, and undesirable. The mere appearance of a larger Black woman's body raises the old Mammy trope that emerged out of a racist, sexist, white male supremacist construct designed to oppress and use Black women's bodies for economic benefit.

Often marginalized and ignored for varying reasons—classism, colorism, racism, and sexism—Lizzo's ratchet womanist act reclaimed large Black women's bodies as beautiful, acceptable, sexual, and fully human. She gave the ultimate middle finger to the respectability police who believe that women like her do not deserve protection because they stand outside of what is subjectively considered superior. Lizzo's actions bring women like herself front and center. Lizzo was free to be herself, dance in public, and cuss out her critics online. She subverted the white gaze that consistently tells Black women and girls that they are never smart, pretty, or capable enough no matter what they do or where they come from. Lizzo loved herself out loud and demanded that she be respected as a human being, whether you liked her or not. In her response on Twitter, she said that she was not going to silence herself:

> Never let someone stop you or shame you for being yourself . . . if you really really don't like my ass you can kiss it. Cause kissing it makes it go away. I promise. Nothing breaks my joy . . . I know that I'm shocking because I know that in a long time you've never seen a body like mine doing whatever it wants to do and dressing the way that it dresses and moving the ways that it moves . . . I'm not going to shrink herself because somebody thinks she's not sexy to them. Bitch, you really think because someone on Twitter think that I'm not cute, I'm gonna stop existing?[5]

You may see Lizzo twerking, but what she is actually doing is protesting the ways in which Black women's bodies are policed; she is embracing her chosen modes of pleasure and joy. In that moment, she is embodying a pleasure politics that acts against white patriarchal norms and domination embraced by respectability politics, which limits Black women's liberative efforts. Moreover, it is a tool to see the humanity and advocacy for all Black women no matter the dynamic. If one is not careful, you will miss the ways she is modeling a form of agency that is available to all kinds of people who are accustomed to being silenced by superficial standards rooted in white supremacy. Finally, you will miss the risk of being seen and heard, but there is danger in being visible. There resides the danger of being criticized, shamed, and ostracized. At the same time, there is the beauty of being seen, heard, and deconstructing systems, in real time, that are violent and harmful toward Black women.

Ratchet womanism recognizes that it is important to have a myriad of representations that creates space for everyone to exist and express their authentic selves. Ratchetness is a radically creative and embodied disrespectability politic that believes Black women should bring their whole selves into every moment by rejecting restrictive standards of behaviors and intercultural policing. It embraces the language and acts that everyday Black women use to push back against the micro- and macroaggressions they experience. Ratchet womanism embraces the art of throwing shade, a good read, and all the nuanced ways Black folks communicate.[6] Black women are also powerful, explosive, imaginative, and defiant and have no boundaries. As such, ratchet womanism pushes back against expectations of acceptable Black womanhood that are too rigid,[7] reductive, restrictive, and conformist.

In the same way that ratchetness emerged out of a specific cultural context from everyday folks, womanism emerged as a response from Black women to the oppression they face and the ordinary solutions they devised and utilized to solve problems. Ratchet womanism is the next level of womanism in that it is modernized for the next generation of Black women and girls. It tells them that they do not have to be like Lizzo, Cardi B, or Michelle Obama in order to be influential or a revolutionary thinker. They can be one of them or all of them, and they still matter. They can be themselves and make a difference in their unique way and not remain beholden to the binaries of black womanhood inherited through respectability politics. It gives women and girls with names like LaKisha, Quintanna, and LaDasha the courage to speak up and out when their names are mispronounced, as they will not accept this form of disrespect. Additionally, while womanism makes space for restoration and forgiveness of the oppressor, ratchet womanism tells the oppressor to go to hell and holds no space for them. Ratchet womanism says that perfunctory forgiveness without deed is all performance and no substance.

Womanist Influence

Womanism is interested in the real lives of everyday Black women, and it provides a lens to examine the underlying power dynamics that lead to them being perceived as an object rather than the subject in a white patriarchal culture. Womanism helps to provide the framework for Black women to name and affirm themselves as women of African descent who have been denied their rightful place in the history of humanity.[8] Womanism recognizes Black women's voices, validates their experiences, and forces the hearers of women's stories to get to know them, thus reducing the "us and them" binaries[9] that contribute to subordination, oppression, and negativity.

Womanism creates space for Black women to engage in willful, outrageous, and audacious agentive practices that reclaim space for themselves. Their actions demonstrate a womanist commitment to ensuring that Black women become actively engaged in their empowerment. Individual empowerment, combined with collective action, leads to transformation. Their transformative power extends to communal change and collective action against patriarchal domination, abuse, and economic and political disenfranchisement. Combining agentive practices, ratchetness, and womanism is key to building subversive, imaginative languages and actions to counter deficient narratives about Black women.

Furthermore, it is a survival strategy of resistance that helps future generations of Black women and girls not just survive but thrive. Black women have learned that engaging in anti-respectability methodologies such as ratchet womanism frees them to explore new ways of expressing their civic and personal demands that cannot be ignored or silenced. Ratchet womanism is loud, hyper-visible, agentive, and not risk-averse. It does not care about the white gaze and its attempt to render Black women unworthy or any attempt to ask them to assimilate in order to be heard and seen.

Levels of Ratchetness

Ratchet womanism works on several levels. First, it allows Black women; however, they present themselves to be heard when they speak authentically without judgment. Respectability politics forces Black women to wear a mask to reflect the ideals and mores of the broader culture. They are often expected to hide their true selves behind the mask of acceptable femininity and not feed into the larger hegemonic discourse about their bodies and sexuality. Ratchet womanism insists on Black women using their voice and body to transform knowledge building for themselves. It is a valid, organic way of questioning, challenging, interrogating, and talking back to oppressive systems that insist on being heard. It dismantles the ways that respectability politics pathologizes poor and working-class women and builds alliances across beliefs so that lessons can be learned from everyone. It is a reminder that lessons for survival come from unexpected places. Ratchet womanism uses Black women's embodied knowledge and positions them as empowered agents in their own liberation.

Second, a ratchet womanist framework gives Black women room for an excessive creativity that leads to a form of hyper-visibility that cannot be missed. Black women have learned that assimilation has not led to their protection. Assimilation has contributed to their invisibility. Despite Black women's achievements, according to the dictates of respectability, they are consistently confronted by violent structures that seek to silence and shame them. Embracing the radical subjectivity of ratchet womanism dismisses the narrow definitions of Black womanhood and leaves room for creating definitions that are powerful and affirming. It resists inter- and intracultural policing of Black women. Ratchet womanism embraces and encourages an over-the-top, rebellious female agency that gives Black women space to express their creativity through excessive responses.

A Twist in Respectability

In an intracultural setting, it looks like the former first lady of the United States (FLOTUS) Michelle Obama, a Black woman who comes from a two-parent home, is a graduate of two prestigious Ivy League institutions, and is married with two children, is the poster child for respectability. Despite her academic and professional achievements, she was still connected to the tropes of hypersexuality, the Jezebel, and the angry black woman, Sapphire. She was referred to as President Barack Obama's "baby mama," a derogatory term referring to children born outside of marriage, and it also implies that she is a difficult, bothersome woman.[10] It was a way of connecting her to a racist legacy of Black women being sexually immoral while ignoring the rapes that forced motherhood on Black women. The "Angry Black Woman" trope was launched when Obama critiqued this country's racism while simultaneously acknowledging her pride in being an American citizen. The July 21, 2008, cover of *The New Yorker* attempted to solidify this Angry Black Woman image by portraying her as a gun-toting, afro-wearing, Black radical, and President Barak Obama as a Black Muslim. The Jezebel trope image was unmasked by the way the media dissected and discussed her body. Articles were written about her sleeveless tops and her behind, which were seen as overtly sexual and distractions to powerful men.[11]

Despite these assaults, Obama insisted on being her most authentic self, and in doing so, she challenged the racist and sexist narratives that sought to reduce her to a stereotype. She engaged in a radical subjectivity that resisted the inter- and intracultural policing that often happens to Black women. The former FLOTUS was not ashamed of her distinctive Black woman's body and all of the attributes and anxieties it evokes. As first lady, she was able to project this message in front of an audience at all times. She rejected the ways in which patriarchy attempts to use women's bodies as a source of shame and silencing. The "side-eye" that she often gave those who attempted to reduce her also communicated her disapproval and for folks to "not let these degrees fool them." She demonstrated that it was okay for Black women to love themselves as they are and not allow people to reduce them to stereotypes. Obama engaged in ratchet womanism. She practiced a Disrespectability politic that refuses to let Black women be shamed for being their most authentic selves.

Moreover, black women's agency affirms the ways they show up in the world and legitimizes their daily resistance activities as normative, valuable, and authoritative—on the grounds that excessive creativity and response are part of the pedagogical impetus of ratchet womanism. Everyone has a seat at the table, regardless of class status, to share resistance strategies and epistemologies that help them navigate and survive in a world hostile to Black women. In this way, it engages in a nonhierarchical, communal womanist discourse where all voices are welcome. All bodies and voices are not the same, and they do not have to agree. However, there is room for them to be supported, respected, and encouraged to achieve freedom and liberation in an effort to end oppression and vulnerability.

Third, ratchet womanism commands and demands an audience so that Black women are seen and heard outside of patriarchal hegemonic discourses that silence those deemed unworthy. It rejects patriarchy's use of women's bodies to render women invisible and unworthy in public and private spaces. Ratchet womanism resists the dampening of Black women's authenticity so others are comfortable; it intentionally names, claims, and shouts the complexities of Black womanhood as a critical consciousness. The voice of their politics, this critical consciousness, positions their identities as antagonistic toward stereotypes, defiant against discrimination, and even dangerous in the face of disrespect. Black women's joy and pain are on full display in ways that cannot be missed or ignored. It is a way to recreate and recenter one's own narrative that is close to one's experience. Ratchet womanism calls on Black women to use their voices, music, dancing, and any other means at their disposal to move from places of pain and silence to power. These are coping strategies that illustrate a creative resistance to how the larger culture attempts to erase them; they are full-bodied expressions of their humanity. Ratchet womanism insists that Black women articulate and demonstrate an understanding of themselves and proclaim their truth.

In Conclusion: The Liberative Standard

Ratchetness is a liberative construct for Black women to combat marginalization and oppressive tropes. Furthermore, it is important to note that not all ratchet behaviors are liberative; there is a standard. There are four important practices to remember. First, engaging in ratchet womanism means that Black women are not complicit with oppression. Black women work together to alleviate the racism, sexism, classism, heterosexism, and other problems that conspire against communities of color.

Second, ratchet womanism is not judgmental or does not engage in the politics of exclusion that isolates Black women because of their appearance, the way they wear their hair, how they dress, or how they earn money to support themselves and their families. It is a framework that meets Black women where they are and encourages dialogue. As a disrespectability politic, ratchet womanism recognizes the tensions of living in a racist, sexist, and classist society that looks to mute Black women's pain, voices, and experiences.

Third, ratchet womanism is not dehumanizing. It confronts the tradition of dehumanization that negatively impacts the quality of life for others. It sees the humanity in every person and works to help people claim their own unique agency to dismantle systems of domination. As a resistant consciousness, it provides a counternarrative that advocates for the healing and preservation of Black girls and women to deconstruct the narratives of white hegemony. Black women draw upon their own language to push back against the micro- and macroaggressions they experience. In this way, they create the necessary discourse and dialogue to collectively decide how to respond.

Fourth, ratchet womanism uses the threat of violence to remove oneself from physically and/or emotionally abusive situations to protect oneself from harm. Engaging in ratchetness for vengeance is not enough. Vengeance is not liberative because it causes more oppression. Ratchet womanism is about dismantling oppression. Actions that do not embody these concepts are outside its liberative framework and become trifling. Trifling acts are self-serving, are not helpful for the larger community, do not work toward the growth of the self in healthy ways, and lack a liberative edge. Ratchet womanist acts are not about performance; it is about how Black women teach each other to challenge sexist, racist, homophobic, and classist ideologies. This embodied knowledge positions them as empowered agents in their own liberation. Ratchet womanism is a reminder that Black women have always checked on themselves and their communities.

RATCHET WOMANISM AND THE
BELOVED COMMUNITY

The term "Beloved Community" is a reference to Martin Luther King Jr.'s goal of communal justice. The Beloved Community for him was a realistic, achievable goal that could be attained by a critical mass of people committed to and trained in the philosophy and methods of nonviolence.[12] This movement is about building spaces of Black freedom and an understanding of

Black people as disenfranchised political and social captives struggling for liberation in a white supremacist society. For King, love and radical acceptance was the route toward ending the suffering of marginalized Black people in every area of American life. What this idea of radical acceptance of the disenfranchised does not ask is what happens when you are subject to inter- and intracommunal violence because of your social status, sartorial choices, educational level, and modes of personal expression? When Black women question the hegemonic norms that govern their appearance, language, and identities that marginalize them and keep them outside of the Beloved Community, how do they ask about their suffering, advocate for themselves, and demand that their humanity is recognized?

Enter teenager Claudette Colvin; she embodies ratchet womanism. In 1955, at the age of fifteen, Colvin refused to give up her seat on the bus in Montgomery, Alabama, and was arrested. Colvin protested her removal, stating her right to sit where she wanted. She demanded not only that her humanity be recognized but that she had the rights and privileges as she, too, was an American citizen. Colvin was a dark-skinned, poor Black girl who was pregnant by a much older man.[13] Colvin was not the image of Black womanhood the movement was calling for and not necessarily welcome into the Beloved Community. Rosa Parks became the face of the Civil Rights Movement when she was arrested for the same act months later. Parks was a married woman, highly respected, and part of strategic planning committees for the movement. She was light-skinned and had "good hair." She represented the kind of Black womanhood the movement could stand behind because her image was beyond reproach. Parks' image was the perfect mélange of respectability politics that conveyed a particular class, color, privilege, and appeal to White allies that was important to the Movement. Parks embodied the Beloved Community, and the choice of Parks over Colvin illustrated that one group of Black women was acceptable, and another group was not. Colvin was of the latter.

Colvin was seen as too emotional, mouthy, and all too imperfect to put at the center of the cause[14] because of her identity. There is a particular kind of Black womanhood that had to be represented, and it was not a pregnant teenager. It looks like Parks, married, and representative of a "quiet dignity" that the movement wanted to project about Black women. It does not get to look like Fannie Lou Hamer, a loud, overweight, dark-skinned, outspoken Black woman who lacked a formal education. It looks like Diane Nash, young, light-skinned, pretty, and smart.

Women like Colvin and Hamer are the antithesis of respectability politics and the image of Black womanhood unwelcome in the Beloved Community. A pregnant teenager raises the specter of Jezebel—the loose, lascivious, hypersexualized Black woman. Hamer fits the stereotypical racist image of

Black womanhood—the Mammy and Sapphire. The movement wanted to put forward these soft yet strong women and utilized their physical, mental, emotional, and spiritual labor and simultaneously disappearing them. The way that the movement chose to parade Black women was problematic and dismissive. Certain people are welcome, and others are not. The Beloved Community judges the worthiness of people. Ratchet womanism reminds us that it takes all kinds of Black womanhood to make a community work.

Dismissing these voices based on appearances causes a deficit in the community. The perception of the ratchet from those within the respectability politic mindset is that they are not honored because they do not have anything worthwhile to offer. Adherents of respectability—the Beloved Community—act as if wisdom does not reside in the margins and is not worthy of being brought to the center. When King talks about the Beloved Community and his expectations, he did not fully explore how gender and respectability politics played a role.

RATCHET WOMANISM CLAPS BACK AT RESPECTABILITY POLITICS AND THE BELOVED COMMUNITY

If we are talking about how love and justice reign, we have to examine how sexism and colorism exist and the underlying assumptions about how those in positions of power and privilege give it dominance. There are protections that privilege offers, and they are not readily conceded. Colvin represented the women on the ground doing the work that funded the movement and put their bodies on the line. Everyday women and their work are seen as an afterthought, and their existence highlights the idea of the necessity of Black women to suffer in order for their contributions to count. Ratchet womanism rejects that narrative. It will not allow other people to say that Black women need to suffer; ratchet womanism will neither ennoble nor enable that narrative.

The Beloved Community and respectability politics uphold dangerous narratives about Black womanhood. Both ideologies dictate who deserves protection, respect, and acceptance based on a performance of femininity rooted in a racist and sexist standard of womanhood. Implicit within the Beloved Community and respectability politics is the idea that one has to prove their humanity, their worthiness to participate and be recognized in society. Ratchet womanism refuses to acquiesce to the demand that Black women accept an oppressive system that continues to demean them even when it is their own community that perpetuates harmful myths. Both the Beloved Community and respectability politics neglect discussions on how structural forces such as race, class, and gender discrimination[15] hinder the health and well-being of Black women and Black people. Ratchet womanism declares, "Miss me with the bullshit! You don't get to disappear me and render me unworthy in public and private spaces because I don't look the part. I belong here! And, if you don't like it, that's your problem, not mine." And in the words of Lizzo, "If you really don't like it, you can kiss my ass."

Colvin demonstrated what it looks when Black women actively speak themselves out of the margins and into the center of their own narratives, which indicts the very institutions that demand their collusion with their oppression. She utilized her voice and her body as a tool to make herself visible, speak herself into existence, and demands that others see how she and other Black women like herself live. Colvin's ratchet womanism challenges the dominant norms around Black womanhood prevalent in the Black community about feminine comportment. It encourages other women to explode the narrow binaries that have complicated their lives.[16] Additionally, Colvin rejected the politics of exclusion that accompanies respectability politics.

RATCHET WOMANISM: A LIBERATORY FRAMEWORK FOR ALL BLACK WOMEN

Ratchet womanism continues to be a reminder that it takes all kinds of Black women to participate in the liberation of the entire community. Ratchet womanism asks the question, "If you're not liberating everyone, are you really talking about freedom?" As an anti-oppressionist ideology and practice, ratchet womanism identifies with liberation projects of all sorts and supports the liberation of all humankind from all forms of oppression.[17] It affirms the voices and gifts of Black women and is an option for those concerned about justice. Ratchet womanists are moved to act beyond the paradigms of race, class, and gender. They are committed to the dignity of all people and recognize that there are several sites of brilliance within the community.

Second, ratchet womanism's emphasis on safe spaces continues to be necessary for Black women. In the midst of community, the well-being of all members becomes the center of concern. There is room for reconciliation and balancing relationships. Developing resilient individuals contributes to building resilient, enduring communities. By aggregating and articulating individual expressions of consciousness, a focused collective consciousness becomes possible.[18] There is room for the single mother and the university professor, the sex worker and the banker, the grandmother and the high school sophomore. Black women need these spaces for knowledge creation, community building, and self-definition.

Finally, ratchet womanism encourages Black women to love themselves. Black women loving themselves pose a threat to heteropatriarchy and white supremacist structures because of their fierceness, beauty, intellect, and fortitude.[19] Encouraging Black women to love themselves means that they are committed to focusing on and exposing injustices that affect marginalized people. As Black women love themselves, they eschew the narrative of a culture that devalues their bodies and beauty. By embracing their aesthetic choices, their creativity offers a template for resistance in a culture that worships at the altar of white beauty standards.

And seriously, did you really think ratchet womanists were going to stop existing because someone didn't like them? Girl bye!

NOTES

1. Bettina Love, "A Ratchet Lens: Black Queer Youth, Agency, Hip Hop and the Black Ratchet Imagination," *Educational Researcher* 46, no. 9 (December 2017): 540.

2. Teresa Fry-Brown, *God Don't Like Ugly: African American Women Handing on Spiritual Values* (Nashville: Abingdon Press, 1989), 173.

3. Mona Eltahawy, *The Seven Necessary Sins for Women and Girls* (Boston: Beacon Press, 2019), 61.

4. Lisa Respers France, *CNN*, Lizzo Twerked in a Thong at a Lakers Game and It Was a Moment, CNN.com. December 10, 2019. https://www.cnn.com/2019/12/10/entertainment/lizzo-thong-trnd/index.html (accessed March 28, 2020).

5. Lizzo Addresses Twerking in a Thong at NBA Lakers Game https://youtu.be/4DKw5Tr46KE (accessed March 28, 2020).

6. Montinique McEachern, "Respect My Ratchet: The Liberatory Consciousness of Ratchetness," *Qualitative Departures in Qualitative Research* 6, no. 3 (Fall 2017): 80.

7. Brittney Cooper, "(Un)Clutching My Mother's Pearls, or Ratchetness and the Residue of Respectability," in *The Crunk Feminist Collective*, eds. Brittney Cooper, Susana Morris, and Robin Bylorn (New York: Feminist Press, 2017), 217.

8. Diana L. Hayes, *Standing in the Shoes My Mother Made: A Womanist Theology* (Minneapolis: Fortress Press, 2011), 3.

9. Stacy Floyd-Thomas, *Deeper Shades of Purple: Womanism in Society and Religion*, ed. Stacy Floyd Thomas (New York: New York University Press, 1999), 4.

10. Melissa Harris-Perry, *Sister Citizen: Shame Stereotypes, and Black Women in America* (New Haven: Yale University Press, 2011), 273.

11. Ibid., 278.

12. The Beloved Community, https://thekingcenter.org/king-philosophy/.

13. Janell Ross, Washington Post, Rosa Parks Is the Name You Know, Claudette Colvin Is the Name You Probably Should, Washington Post December 1, 2015 https

::/www.washingtonpost.com/news/the-fix/wp/2015/12/01/rosa-parks-the-name-you
-know-claudette-colvin-the-one-too-many-dont/ (accessed March 27, 2020).

14. Ross, Washington Post.

15. Frederick Harris, "The Rise of Respectability Politics," *Dissent Magazine* Winter 2014: 34.

16. Love, "A Ratchet Lens," 539.

17. Layli Phillips, *The Womanist Reader* (New York: Routledge, 2006), xxiv.

18. Janice D. Hamlet, "Assessing Womanist Thought: The Rhetoric of Susan L. Taylor," in *The Womanist Reader*, ed. Layli Phillips (New York: Routledge, 2006), 226.

19. Brittney Cooper, Susana Morris, and Robin Bylorn, "Sisterhood: She's Not Heavy, She's My Sister," in *The Crunk Feminist Collective*, eds. Brittney Cooper, Susana Morris, and Robin Bylorn (New York: The Feminist Press: 2017), 270.

BIBLIOGRAPHY

Cooper, Brittney, Susana Morris, and Robin Boylorn. "Sisterhood: She's Not Heavy, She's My Sister." in *The Crunk Feminist Collective*. Edited by Brittney Cooper, Susana Morris, and Robin Bylorn, 269–272. New York: The Feminist Press, 2017.

_____. "(Un)Clutching My Mother's Pearls, or Ratchetness and the Residue of Respectability." In *The Crunk Feminist Collective*. Edited by Brittney Cooper, Susana Morris, and Robin Bylorn, 201–204. New York: Feminist Press, 2017.

Eltahawy, Mona. *The Seven Necessary Sins for Women and Girls*. Boston: Beacon Press, 2019.

Floyd-Thomas, Stacy. *Deeper Shades of Purple: Womanism in Society and Religion*. Edited by Stacy Floyd Thomas. New York: New York University Press, 1999.

Fry-Brown, Teresa. *God Don't Like Ugly: African American Women Handing on Spiritual Values*. Nashville: Abingdon Press, 1989.

Hamlet, Janice D. "Assessing Womanist Thought: The Rhetoric of Susan L. Taylor." In *The Womanist Reader*. Edited by Layli Phillips, 215–230. New York: Routledge, 2006.

Harris, Frederick. "The Rise of Respectability Politics." *Dissent Magazine* (Winter 2014): 33–37.

Harris-Perry, Melissa. *Sister Citizen: Shame, Stereotypes, and Black Women in America*. New Haven: Yale, 2011.

Hayes, Diana L. *Standing in the Shoes My Mother Made: A Womanist Theology*. Minneapolis: Fortress Press, 2011.

Love, Bettina. "A Ratchet Lens: Black Queer Youth, Agency, Hip Hop and the Black Ratchet Imagination." *Educational Researcher* 46, no. 9 (December 2017): 539–547.

McEachern, Montinique. "Respect My Ratchet: The Liberatory Consciousness of Ratchetness." *Qualitative Departures in Qualitative Research* 6, no. 3 (Fall 2017): 78–89.

Phillips, Layli. *The Womanist Reader*. New York: Routledge, 2006.

Richardson, Allissa V. "Dismantling Respectability: The Rise of New Womanist Communication Models in the Era of Black Lives Matter." *Journal of Communication* 69 (April 2019): 193–213.

Ross, Janell. "Rosa Parks Is the Name You Know, Claudette Colvin Is the Name You Probably Should," *WashingtonPost.com*. https://www.washingtonpost.com/news/the-fix/wp/2015/12/01/rosa-parks-the-name-you-know-claudette-colvin-the-one-too-many-dont/. Accessed March 27, 2020.

Smith, Mychal Denzel, Brittney Cooper, Khalil Gilbran Mohammed, and Randall Robinson. *Stage for Debate: Respectability and Activism Schomburg Center for Research in Black Culture*. New York, New York February 2, 2016.

The Beloved Community, https://thekingcenter.org/king-philosophy/.

Chapter 6

"Women, Step Forward!"

Doing Rhetorical Historiography by Exploring Womanist Leadership in the AME Church

Natonya Listach and Andre E. Johnson

In a denomination with two female bishops (one who will retire in 2020; the other in 2024), the African Methodist Episcopal (AME) Church seems to be progressive in the trajectory of women's roles in the church. However, there is still more work to do as women's voices are continuously bombarded, overlooked, or even pushed out of the conversation. With this in mind, how can women work to advance their position in the denomination? While some men, such as Bishop Henry McNeal Turner, fought for the inclusion of women in every aspect of the leadership of the AME Church, the seeds of inclusion were planted, watered, and harvested by the women of the denomination. This chapter will focus on historical examples of women pushing forth as rhetors in the AME Church—Jarena Lee, Sarah (Sallie) Ann Copeland Hughes, Hallie Quinn Brown, and Jamye Coleman Williams.

To understand the trajectory of female leadership in the AME Church, one must first understand the history of the AME Church. Established in 1816, the AME Church was formed because of racial discrimination toward African Americans at St. George's Methodist Episcopal Church in Philadelphia.[1] Richard Allen (the first bishop of the AME Church)[2] and Absalom Jones (the first African American ordained priest in the United States)[3] were preachers for the African American members of St. George. They had been instrumental in increasing their membership in the congregation. However, the increase in African American membership displeased the white congregation and led to the segregation of African American members from the white worshippers. After an attempted relocation from the main floor of the church to the gallery, Allen, Jones, and the other African American members walked out of the service and formed the Free African Society, which eventually split into The African Church, with Jones as the leader, and Bethel A.M.E. Church, with Allen serving as pastor.

Yet the formation and success of the AME Church were not dependent on Richard Allen alone. Sara (or Sarah) Allen, his wife, continuously supported Allen's ministry by forming the Daughters of the Conference, a network of AME women who "mended the garments of the ministers, gave them food, and provided them with the material support they needed to survive."[4] This group would later become the Women's Missionary Society, and their scope would expand from just assisting local ministers into helping people through-out the world.[5] Unknown to them at the time, by working within the political structure of the church, these "Daughters of the Conference" set the founda-tion for the emergence of womanist theology and established an environment for women to take on leadership roles in the church's hierarchical structure.

It would seem to follow that in a denomination that is willing to acknowl-edge the abilities of both men and women to serve in leadership positions, womanist theology would be welcome in their beliefs. As defined by Debra Washington and cited in Kate Coleman's article, womanist theology focuses on the liberation of African American women by centering itself on African American women.[6] Therefore, womanist theology is grounded in the advance-ment of African American women in which the AME Church played a part.

The AME Church's unification of Methodist rules, which follow "a plain and simple gospel" and Episcopalian governmental structure, with bishops governing the global organization of churches, provided a structure that would eventually favor the inclusion of women in leadership.[7] This structure allowed the denomination to benefit from a unique political structure that consisted of leaders in both the AME Church and the African American community. The African American leadership consisted of a group of the "black elite" who "developed political rhetoric of equality and liberty that was strongly rooted in the American revolutionary tradition and biblical moral conventions."[8] This democratic organization, with diverse political affiliations and ideologies, laid the foundation for women to begin presenting themselves as viable candidates for ordination as pastors in the AME Church.

JARENA LEE

Debates over the inclusion of women in pastoral roles preceded the formation of the AME Church; the denomination's framework of equality and liberty led directly to the debate over the inclusion of women in pastoral positions, with Richard Allen's rejection of Jarena Lee's calling to the ministry. Lee joined the AME Church after hearing Allen preach and received her calling from God to preach in 1807.[9] Unfortunately, due to the AME Church's ban of women ministers, Allen overruled her calling, noting the laws of the church would only allow women to conduct prayer meetings and become exhorters[10] but not pastors of the church. Lee confided in her journal, "[i]f the man may preach, because the Saviour [*sic*] died for him, why not the woman? seeing [*sic*] he died for her also. Is he not a whole Saviour, [*sic*] instead of a half one? as [*sic*] those who hold it wrong for a woman to preach, [*sic*] would seem to make it appear."[11]

Lee placed her calling on hold. During this time, she married Pastor Joseph Lee, had two children, and served as an exhorter for the church.[12] Yet, the Lord's calling would return.

After the death of her husband, she attended a church service where the minister froze during his sermon and stated in her journal:

> in the same instant, I sprang, as by altogether supernatural impulse, to my feet, when I was aided from above to give an exhortation on the very text which my brother Williams had taken.
>
> I told them I was like Jonah; for it had been then nearly eight years since the Lord had called me to preach his gospel to the fallen sons and daughters of Adam's race, but that I had lingered like him and delayed to go at the bidding of the Lord, and warn those who are as deeply guilty as were the people of Ninevah.
>
> During the exhortation, God made manifest his power in a manner sufficient to show the world that I was called to labor according to my ability, and the grace given unto me, in the vineyard of the good husbandman.[13]

Lee's confidence in her calling to the ministry, as well as her dedication to the AME Church, ultimately persuaded Allen to support Lee's calling to the ministry. Although Allen licensed Lee to preach, Lee was not allowed to be ordained.[14] Even though her calling was "legitimized" in the eyes of a male leadership figure, the church's hierarchal structure denied her the ability to become a full preacher in the AME Church.

While her ministry did not specifically focus on African American women, her focus on a God who called both men and women to preach showed the beginnings of a womanist theology. Lee's dedication to God, as well as to the AME Church, would broaden by the next generation of African American women.

SARAH (SALLIE) ANN COPELAND HUGHES

Much of the life and legacy of Sarah (Sallie) Ann Copeland Hughes has been lost to history, but we do know that she was born in 1847 in Wake

County, North Carolina. "Copeland Hughes was a member of a community of educated, free, and free-born Black women who were called to preach and teach in the Black church."[15] Although we do not know exactly when she started, Copeland Hughes became a "well-known evangelist in her home state of North Carolina."[16] In November of 1861, at the age of fourteen, she conducted a service at the church's Annual Conference Session, indicating that as an evangelist, her "preaching talent was recognized and validated." However, as noted by Burgher:

> Evangelists were not assigned to a church or given the responsibility of a congregation. Free-floating, evangelists and lay preachers were invited to serve as needed. For Copeland Hughes, this meant that men who were given charge of churches' budgets and congregations, to which she had no access, had to invite her. Regardless, Copeland Hughes made a name for herself.[17]

At the North Carolina Annual Conference in 1882, the church, recognizing her gifts and abilities, appointed Copeland Hughes to a church in Fayetteville, North Carolina. Over the next two years, she would fill pastorates in Wilson's Mills and in Charlotte, North Carolina. Moving from an evangelist to a pastor brought its own set of problems. According to historian Stephen Ward Angell, Copeland Hughes not only had to deal with "pay discrimination" but also had to deal with churches that were not so keen on receiving a woman as pastor. Besides, she also had to deal with the resentment of her male colleagues, who were known to give her the wrong meeting times for important meetings. However, despite all of this, Copeland Hughes's ministry was fruitful. Under her leadership, she built churches, "conducted revivals," and "gained converts." It led one of her contemporaries to note that Copeland Hughes's ministry "has been attended by great power."[18]

Two years later, Copeland Hughes attended the 1884 General Conference in Baltimore with great anticipation. She and five other women expected the church to reaffirm their roles as pastors by now officially licensing them. Although there was some support for the licensing of women pastors and preachers, most of the delegates supported a resolution that would deny women the privilege of licensing. The resolution adopted prohibited women from serving as pastors, meaning that Copeland Hughes had to give up her pastorate. According to Angell, after Copeland Hughes's resignation, instead of continuing to meet as a church, the "saddened congregation" decided to disband and look for church homes elsewhere. Her frustration with the church probably led her not to attend the state Annual Conference later that year. Still, she did attend the North Carolina Annual State Conference the following year in November of 1885.[19]

Members of the conference gave her a warm reception. Fellow ministers greeted her "courteously," and the conference leaders asked her to preach at one of the primary services at 11 a.m. at First Baptist Church. She also offered the closing prayer of the conference but was not given a pastoral assignment for the year 1886. However, in a surprise to her and everyone in attendance, on November 30, 1885, Bishop Henry McNeal Turner ordained her and nine other men as deacons.

As reported in the *New York Times*, she was a "well-educated," "bright mulatto" woman who could preach. When she came around the altar to have the bishop ordain her, "the entire congregation, both white and colored," looked on with intense interest. Finally, after the bishop "halted for some minutes and looked up," apparently as the *New York Times* said in "deep thought," he placed his hands on her head and said, "Take thou authority to execute the office of a deacon in the church of God, in the name of the Father, the Son, and Holy Ghost." After he presented her with a Bible, she rose as having the distinction of becoming the first ordained woman in the AME Church.[20]

Her ordination was short-lived. Two years later, at the 1887 North Carolina Annual Conference, Bishop Jabez Campbell, who presided over the conference that year, ruled that her ordination had been against church law and had her name removed from the list of deacons. In 1888 at the General Conference, the church issued a resolution that repudiated Turner and ended any hope of women's ordinations for the foreseeable future.

> Whereas, Bishop H. M. Turner has seen fit to ordain a woman to the order of a deacon; and Whereas, said act is contrary to the usage of our Church, and without a precedent in any other body of Christians in the known world, and as it cannot be proven by the Scriptures that a woman has ever been ordained to the order of the ministry; Therefore be it enacted, That the bishops of the African Methodist Episcopal Church be and are hereby forbidden to ordain a woman to the order of a deacon or an elder in our Church.[21]

In a span of five years, Copeland Hughes had systematically been forced out of the denomination she not only tirelessly worked for but also loved. By actions of her state and general conferences, Copeland Hughes lost her church and her ordination as a deacon. Her name does not appear in any known AME records after 1888.

HALLIE QUINN BROWN

The AME Church would gain one of its most significant activists with the birth of Hallie Quinn Brown in 1850.[22] Brown, an active member of the AME Church, was introduced to activism by her parents, who used their house as a

part of the Underground Railroad.[23] She continued their fight for equal rights
and eventually became nationally known as a public reader/speaker and advocate for women's rights and civil rights.

Brown's public readings were created to touch the emotions of her audiences. Using pieces from well-known poets and writers of the time, Brown
created presentations that not only educated her audiences but also allowed
them to contemplate the need for equality of African Americans.[24] Brown
spoke before gatherings such as the World's Congress of Representative
Women to ask the group not to ignore the concerns of African American
women while fighting for the rights of white women. In her speech, Brown
spoke passionately about the achievements of African American women and
ended her speech by eloquently stating:

> Talk not of the negro woman's incapacity, of her inferiority, until the centuries
> of her hideous servitude have been succeeded by centuries of education, culture,
> and refinement, by which she may rise to the fullness of the stature of her high-
> est ideal.

God speed the day when the white American woman, strengthened by her
wealth, her social position, and her years of superior training, may clasp
hands with the less fortunate black women of America, and both unite in
declaring that "God hath made of one blood all nations of men for to dwell
on all the face of the earth."[25]

Brown wanted her audience to understand that African American women
were just as smart and capable as their white counterparts. She encouraged
white women to include African American women in their work for equality.

Brown demonstrated her belief in the advocation for women's rights in
the AME Church by becoming a candidate for the office of Secretary of
Education. This role oversaw the implementation of the denomination's
church school.[26] Brown's platform included moving the church education
program to a more inclusive and holistic model that would uplift both women
and men through education, both religious and secular.

Before she took on this task, however, she reached out to Bishop Henry
McNeal Turner for support. Bishop Turner gave her his unwavering support.
In a personal letter addressed to Brown, Turner wrote:

> I say run, and you will get big support. You shall have the Voice of the
> Missions[27] at your back. I will support you with all my might. A powerful argu-
> ment can be made on your behalf. You can tell the church that the women pay in
> more money than the men, that but for the class dues of the women half of our
> ministers would starve to death. You will be able to show that you have done

more in person, to give character to our church and to build up our educational interest, than any secretary of education in the history of the church.

On paper, Brown was a strong candidate for the position. She had taught at Wilberforce University, an AME-owned and -operated school, where she received her Bachelor of Science degree. She was one of the leading elocutionists and orators in America. By the time of her candidacy, she had already written two books and had the endorsement of the senior bishop of the church. However, it was not enough and Brown lost her bid due to the church's hierarchical structure and male leadership.

Both Lee's and Brown's ideals of the rights of African Americans mimicked the ideological trajectory of the AME Church. While Lee advocated for the civil rights of African Americans, Brown focused on increasing the rights of African American women. Brown's ideologies consistently focused on the traditions and practices of African American women and their manifestation in the progress of the African American race as a whole. Yet, to see the inclusion of women in the traditionally male roles of the AME Church, activists would need to continue to strive for higher leadership positions for those women.

JAMYE COLEMAN WILLIAMS

One of the women who sat in Brown's classrooms would carry the fight for equality from the North to the South. Dr. Jamye Coleman Williams studied at Wilberforce University. Eventually, she taught at four AME colleges—Edward Waters College, Shorter College, Morris Brown College, and Wilberforce University—before landing at Tennessee State University.[28] While there, Williams taught students who would become doctors, engineers, college presidents, and bishops in the AME Church. She also served the AME Church as president of the 13th District Lay Organization and editor of the *AME Church Review*. Ultimately she was elected as the first female general officer in the AME Church. In an interview with Larry Crowe, Williams recalled, "when I ran, my sex did not become an issue. And I think it was because of, you know, the friendships I had with all these people and the people who had been our students."[29]

Williams was also an activist, working with various community and civic groups and serving on the Executive Committee of the NAACP for over forty years.[30] She served alongside leaders such as Martin Luther King, Jr., John Lewis, and Thurgood Marshall, striving for civil rights. Her activism was especially important to the denomination as Williams was instrumental in the election of the first female bishop in the AME Church. As the first female campaign manager for a bishop in the AME Church, Williams was known for her knowledge of the church's political structure. She told Crowe during an interview:

> I think a lot of the people thought that, you know, I would be of some help in getting them elected . . . I had promised the women—we have an organization called Women in Ministry, and they had asked me to come to Atlanta [Georgia] to speak at a forum they had. They, what they said to me was, "We have the woman power, but we have not been in the political structure. So we don't know the politics and we need help, and so we want you to help us." So I told them that I would help some women to get elected to the bishopric.[31]

Williams used her knowledge of past AME Church political resolutions to encourage the election of the first female bishop. She knew that the elections of both the first African bishops and the first bishop from the Caribbean occurred because of special resolutions that called for the electorate to set aside one position for those groups presented during the AME Church's General Conference in July of 2000.[32] This proved a difficult fight because the bishops had already decided they would not elect a woman until the next General Conference. Yet, Williams strategically persisted. For months before the General Conference, she spoke consistently about the need for a female bishop in the AME Church. To play toward the patriarchal nature of the AME Church, she deliberately chose a well-known and respected male pastor to present the resolution to the General Conference delegation.

Williams gave a final nudge before the conference voted on the resolution—she told the conference that "they were gon' be just like the Southern Baptist, who will not recognize a woman. And that made folks sort of upset."[33] Ultimately, the resolution failed. However, even though the resolution did not pass, Williams knew that focusing her attention on the resolution and not the election of a specific female bishop would allow the conference to vote on the female candidates based on their own merits. During that same conference, the delegates elected the first female bishop—Vashti Murphy McKenzie.

THE TRAJECTORY OF FEMALE
LEADERSHIP IN THE AME CHURCH

The women of the AME Church have a legacy of women who remained devoted to the AME Church yet persistently challenged its patriarchal hierarchy. As Dodson noted in her book *Engendering Church: Women, Power, and the AME Church*:

There were women who put forth extraordinary individual efforts; women who merged their energies with those of other women; women who were indispensable to Church growth but are yet unknown; women who assertively and consciously worked to be included in the Church, and other women, with more spiritual agendas, for whom structural inclusion was insignificant. But when the entire story of the nineteenth century is told, women are seen to have compelled the denomination to create structural positions for their gender.[34]

Lee, Copeland Hughes, Brown, and Williams demonstrate the tenacity of women in the AME Church. And their legacy has continued into the present generation. Currently, the Connectional AME Women in Ministry is keeping the progression of equality alive by supporting and expanding the role of women in ministry and leadership positions in the AME Church. Their mission notes a sense of pride in the election of three female bishops[35] and one female general officer as well as their desire to "keep pressing to eliminate sexist and discriminatory practices and that we must continue to raise our voices until there are full equity and inclusion of women in ministry in the life, ministry, and leadership of the AME Church."[36]

Overall, the AME Church has made great strides in equality and representation of its female members in leadership positions. These strides include the evolution of a womanist theology woven through the acknowledgment of God's calling to preach on Jarena Lee, the inclusion of Hallie Quinn Brown as a general officer, and the eventual election of their first female bishop, the Reverend Vashti Murphy McKenzie, in the year 2000. Motivated by the ingenuity of Jamye Coleman Williams, the AME Church continues to strive for equality and inclusion of its female members. And through the work of the Connectional AME Women in Ministry, the AME Church will advance the organization's theme of "Standing United, Moving Forward, Stronger Together."[37]

NOTES

1. "Our History," AME Church, The Official African Methodist Episcopal Church Website, accessed August 13, 2019. https://www.ame-church.com/our-church/our-history/.

2. Priscilla Pope-Levison, "Richard Allen [Pennsylvania] (1760-1831)," *BlackPast*, last modified May 02, 2019, https://www.blackpast.org/african-american-history/allen-richard-pennsylvania-1760-1831/.

3. Victor Tolly, "Absalom Jones (1746–1818)," *BlackPast*, last modified August 08, 2019, https://www.blackpast.org/african-american-history/jones-absalom-1746-1818/.

4. "Sara Allen 1764–1849," PBS, accessed August 13, 2019, https://www.pbs .org/wgbh/aia/part3/3p246.html.

5. "A Brief History of the Women's Missionary Society of the African Methodist Episcopal Church," *WMS History, Women's Missionary Society of the African Methodist Episcopal Church*, accessed August 13, 2019, http://www.wms-amec.org/ wms-history.html.

6. Kate Coleman, "Black Theology and Black Liberation: A Womanist Perspective," *Black Theology in Britain: A Journal of Contextual Praxis* 1, no. 1 (October 1998): 8, http://search.ebscohost.com.ezproxy.mtsu.edu/login.aspx?direct =true&db=asn&AN=5654925&site=eds-live&scope=site.

7. "The AME Name," AME Church, the Official African Methodist Episcopal Church Website, accessed August 13, 2019, https://www.ame-church.com/our-chur ch/our-name/.

8. Lawrence Little, *Disciples of Liberty: The African Methodist Episcopal Church in the Age of Imperialism, 1884-1916* (Knoxville: University of Tennessee Press, 2000), 5.

9. Teisha Wilson, "Jarena Lee (1783–185?)," BlackPast, last modified June 29, 2019, https://www.blackpast.org/african-american-history/lee-jarena-1783/.

10. An exhorter is considered a lay member of the AME Church. According to *The Doctrine and Discipline of the African Methodist Episcopal Church 2012*, they should teach the church school and manage and lead prayer meetings. They can speak at their church or other churches but are not considered a pastor.

11. Jarena Lee, "Religious Experience and Journal of Mrs. Jarena Lee, Giving an Account of Her Call to Preach the Gospel," Internet Archive, last modified July 6, 2009, https://archive.org/details/religiousexperi00leegoog/mode/2up, 11.

12. Wilson, "Jarena Lee."

13. Lee, "Religious Experience."

14. "Our Herstory," Connectional AME Women in Ministry, accessed August 13, 2019, http://www.amewim.org/our-herstory.html.

15. Colored Convention Project. Exhibit on Henry McNeal Turner co-curated by Denise Burgher and Andre E. Johnson. https://coloredconventions.org/before-ga rvey-mcneal-turner/black-women-preachers/sarah-hughes-and-black-women-preac hers/ (para 2).

16. Colored Convention Project. Exhibit on Henry McNeal Turner cocurated by Denise Burgher and Andre E. Johnson. https://coloredconventions.org/before-ga rvey-mcneal-turner/black-women-preachers/sarah-hughes-and-black-women-preac hers/ (para 3).

17. Colored Convention Project. Exhibit on Henry McNeal Turner cocurated by Denise Burgher and Andre E. Johnson. https://coloredconventions.org/before-ga rvey-mcneal-turner/black-women-preachers/sarah-hughes-and-black-women-preac hers/ (para 3).

18. Stephen Ward Angell. *Henry McNeal Turner and Black Religion in the South, 1865-1900*. (PhD diss, Vanderbilt University, 1988), 508–509.

19. Angell, *Henry McNeal Turner*, 514.

20. A Female Preacher Ordained. *New York Times*. December 1, 1885.

21. Charles Spencer Smith. A History of the African Methodist Episcopal Church: 1856–1922, Vol. 2 Documenting the American South. https://docsouth.unc.edu/churc h/cssmith/smith.html (159).

22. Ronald Jackson and Sonja Brown Givens, "Hallie Quinn Brown," in *Black Pioneers in Communication Research* (Thousand Oaks, CA: SAGE Publications, Inc, 2006), 65.

23. Yvette Hyter and Judity Duchan, "Hallie Quinn Brown C. 1850–1949," Judy Duchan's History of Speech-Language Pathology, accessed July 15, 2019. https://ww w.acsu.buffalo.edu/~duchan/new_history/hist20c/hallie_brown.html.

24. Jane Donawerth, *Conversational Rhetoric: The Rise and Fall of a Women's Tradition, 1600-1900* (Carbondale, IL: Southern Illinois Univ. Press, 2013).

25. Carrie Chapman Catt and May Wright Sewall, "The World's Congress of Representative Women. [Electronic Resource]: A Historical Râesumâe for Popular Circulation of the World's Congress of Representative Women, Convened in Chicago on May 15, and Adjourned on May 22, 1893, under the Auspices of the Woman's Branch of the World's Congress Auxiliary," in *Women and Social Movements: Scholar's Edition* (Rand, McNally & Company, 1894), http://search.ebscohost.com/lo gin.aspx?direct=true&db=cat00263a&AN=mts.b3363994&site=eds-live&scope=site.

26. Daleah Goodwin, "*'A Torch in the Valley': The Life and Work of Miss Hallie Quinn Brown*" (PhD diss., University of Georgia, 2014), http://purl.galileo.usg.edu/ uga_etd/goodwin_daleah_b_201408_phd, 80.

27. *Voice of Mission* was the newspaper that Turner edited for the church from 1893 to 1900.

28. "Jamye Coleman Williams's Biography," The HistoryMakers, accessed August 2, 2019, https://www.thehistorymakers.org/biography/jamye-coleman-wil liams-39.

29. "Jamye Coleman Williams Talks about Being Elected the First Woman Major General Officer of the A.M.E. Church in 1984," The HistoryMakers, accessed August 2, 2019, https://thmdigital.thehistorymakers.org/story/178474;cID=A2003.18 7;type=1.

30. Alice Bernstein, "Dr. Jamye Coleman Williams: A Passion for Education and Justice," *Tennessee Tribune*, May 5, 2016, http://allianceofethicsandart.org/images/ Index page images/Dr Jamye Coleman Williams_A Passion For Justice_reprint_May 5_2016-optimized.pdf.

31. "Jamye Coleman Williams Recalls Introducing a Resolution Which Was the Catalyst for Electing the First A.M.E. Woman Bishop, HistoryMaker Vashti McKenzie, Pt. 1," *The HistoryMakers*, accessed August 2, 2019, https://thmdigital.t hehistorymakers.org/story/178475.

32. HistoryMakers, "Jamye Coleman Williams Recalls."

33. "Jamye Coleman Williams Recalls Introducing a Resolution Which Was the Catalyst for Electing the First A.M.E. Woman Bishop, HistoryMaker Vashti McKenzie, Pt. 3," *The HistoryMakers*, accessed August 2, 2019, https://thmdigital.t hehistorymakers.org/story/178383.

34. Jualynne Dodson, *Engendering Church: Women, Power, and the AME Church* (Lanham, MD: Rowman & Littlefield, 2002), 4.

35. "The AME Church Elects More Women Bishops: New African Leadership Too. Accessed June 7, 2020, https://www.christiancentury.org/article/2004-07/ame -church-elects-more-women-bishops. Vashti Murphy McKenzie elected in 2000, Carolyn Tyler Guidry and Sarah Francis Davis both elected in 2004.

36. AME Women in Ministry, "Our Herstory."

37. "Connectional AME Women in Ministry," Connectional AME Women in Ministry, accessed August 13, 2019, http://www.amewim.org/home.html.

BIBLIOGRAPHY

Bernstein, Alice. "Dr. Jamye Coleman Williams: A Passion for Education and Justice." *Tennessee Tribune*. May 5, 2016. http://allianceofethicsandart.org/image s/Index page images/Dr Jamye Coleman Williams_A Passion For Justice_reprint_ May 5_2016-optimized.pdf.

Catt, Carrie Chapmanand May Wright Sewall. "The World's Congress of Representative Women. [Electronic Resource]: A Historical Râesumâe for Popular Circulation of the World's Congress of Representative Women, Convened in Chicago on May 15, and Adjourned on May 22, 1893, under the Auspices of the Woman's Branch of the World's Congress Auxiliary." In *Women and Social Movements: Scholar's* Edition. Rand, McNally & Company, 1894. http://search.e bscohost.com/login.aspx?direct=true&db=cat00263a&AN=mts.b3363994&site= eds-live&scope=site.

Christian Century, "The AME Church Elects More Women Bishops: New African Leadership Too. Accessed June 7, 2020, https://www.christiancentury.org/article /2004-07/ame-church-elects-more-women-bishops.

Coleman, Kate. "Black Theology and Black Liberation: A Womanist Perspective." *Black Theology in Britain: A Journal of Contextual Praxis* 1, no. 1 (October 1998): 1–10. http://search.ebscohost.com.ezproxy.mtsu.edu/login.aspx?direct=true&db =asn&AN=5654925&site=eds-live&scope=site.

Colored Convention Project exhibit on Henry McNeil Turner, co-curated by Denise Burgher and Andre E. Johnson. The map displaying newspaper coverage of the convention was created by Samantha DeVera. Created for Dr. P. Gabrielle Foreman's History/English 641 class, Spring 2016. Edited by P. Gabrielle Foreman and Sarah Patterson. Acknowledgements: Samantha de Vera, Simone Austin, Kelli Coles, and Caleb Trotter for further edits, visualization contributions, and technical assistance. Last accessed: July 17, 2020. http://coloredconventions.org/exhibits/s how/bishophmturner/hmturnerconventions/turnersconvention-1893.

Connectional AME Women In Ministry. "Connectional AME Women in Ministry." Accessed August 13, 2019. http://www.amewim.org/home.html.

Connectional AME Women in Ministry. "Our Herstory." Accessed August 13, 2019. http://www.amewim.org/our-herstory.html.

Dodson, Jualynne. *Engendering Church: Women, Power, and the AME Church.* Lanham, MD: Rowman & Littlefield, 2002.

Donawerth, Jane. *Conversational Rhetoric: The Rise and Fall of a Women's Tradition, 1600-1900.* Carbondale, IL: Southern Illinois Univ. Press, 2013.

Goodwin, Daleah. "'*A Torch in the Valley': The Life and Work of Miss Hallie Quinn Brown.*" PhD diss., University of Georgia, 2014. http://purl.galileo.usg.edu/ug a_etd/goodwin_daleah_b_201408_phd.

Hyter, Yvette and Judity Duchan. "Hallie Quinn Brown C. 1850–1949." Judy Duchan's History of Speech-Language Pathology. Accessed July 15, 2019. https:// www.acsu.buffalo.edu/~duchan/new_history/hist20c/hallie_brown.html.

Jackson, Ronald and Sonja Brown Givens. *Black Pioneers in Communication Research.* 64–80. Thousand Oaks, Calif: SAGE Publications, Inc, 2006.

Lee, Jarena. "Religious Experience and Journal of Mrs. Jarena Lee, Giving an Account of Her Call to Preach the Gospel." Internet Archive. Last modified July 6, 2009. https://archive.org/details/religiousexperi00leegoog/mode/2up.

Little, Lawrence. *Disciples of Liberty: The African Methodist Episcopal Church in the Age of Imperialism, 1884-1916.* Knoxville: University of Tennessee Press, 2000.

PBS. "Sara Allen 1764-1849." Accessed August 13, 2019. https://www.pbs.org/ wgbh/aia/part3/3p246.html.

Pope-Levison, Priscilla. "Richard Allen [Pennsylvania] (1760–1831)," BlackPast. Last modified May 2, 2019. https://www.blackpast.org/african-american-history/ allen-richard-pennsylvania-1760-1831/.

The Doctrine and Discipline of the African Methodist Episcopal Church 2012. Nashville, TN: AMEC Sunday School Union, 2012.

The HistoryMakers. "Jamye Coleman Williams Recalls Introducing a Resolution Which Was the Catalyst for Electing the First A.M.E. Woman Bishop, HistoryMaker Vashti McKenzie, Pt. 1." Accessed August 2, 2019. https://thmdigital.thehistorym akers.org/story/178475.

The HistoryMakers. "Jamye Coleman Williams Recalls Introducing a Resolution Which Was the Catalyst for Electing the First A.M.E. Woman Bishop, HistoryMaker Vashti McKenzie, Pt. 3." Accessed August 2, 2019. https://thmdigital.thehistorym akers.org/story/178383.

The HistoryMakers. "Jamye Coleman Williams Talks about Being Elected the First Woman Major General Officer of the AME Church in 1984." Accessed August 2, 2019. https://thmdigital.thehistorymakers.org/story/178474;cID=A2003.187;type=1.

The HistoryMakers, "Jamye Coleman Williams's Biography." Accessed August 2, 2019. https://www.thehistorymakers.org/biography/jamye-coleman-williams-39.

The Official African Methodist Episcopal Church Website, "The AME Name." AME Church. Accessed August 13, 2019. https://www.ame-church.com/our-church/our -name/.

The Official African Methodist Episcopal Church Website. "Our History." AME Church. Accessed August 13, 2019. https://www.ame-church.com/our-church/ou r-history/.

The Official African Methodist Episcopal Church Website. "Our Motto." AME Church. Accessed August 16, 2019. https://www.ame-church.com/our-church/ou r-motto/.

Tolly, Victor. "Absalom Jones (1746-1818)." BlackPast. Last modified August 8, 2019. https://www.blackpast.org/african-american-history/jones-absalom-1746-1818/.

Wilson, Teisha. "Jarena Lee (1783–185?)." BlackPast. Last modified June 29, 2019. https://www.blackpast.org/african-american-history/lee-jarena-1783/.

Women's Missionary Society of the African Methodist Episcopal Church. "A Brief History of the Women's Missionary Society of the African Methodist Episcopal Church." WMS History. Accessed August 13, 2019. http://www.wms-amec.org/wms-history.html.

Chapter 7

"I Am My Sisters' Keeper"

Invitational Rhetoric and Womanist Theology

Tracy Coquette Bass and Michelle Rhnea Yisrael

I took a look in the mirror, whom did I see? Someone who looked a lot like me.
I did not recognize the pain behind my eyes; the
   reflection was mine; I could not hide.
I caught a glimpse of the real me walking by; the mirror reflects, but it never lies.
The mirror often reflects the unexpected; the mess we thought was undetected.
We wear masks to hide from lies; the mirror knows who we are, but try to deny.
So, we avoid the mirror at all costs; we make the conscious decision to remain lost.
Objects in the mirror might seem closer than they appear;
   the mirror is a map that says "You are here."[1]

ORIGINS OF RHETORIC

"In the beginning, God created the heaven and the earth." "And God said, Let there be light: and there was light."[2] The Most High God's first words spoken in protest of the darkness convey the power of rhetoric in written and oral form. Rhetoric encompasses the study of writing or speaking as a means of communication or persuasion and the skills required for the effective use of speech but embodies so much more.[3] In this way, the genetic essence of rhetoric elicits tailored communication,[4] enacted for a specific event or purpose, and embodied through performance.[5] In *The Art of Rhetoric*,[6] Aristotle—known as the "Father of Rhetoric"—defines rhetoric as "demonstration," provoked by the discovery of all "possible means of persuasion."[7] Rhetorician Kenneth Burke, on the other hand, refers to rhetoric as "identification," contending people connect when they identify with the messenger and/or message they receive.[8]

Non-Eurocentric forms of rhetoric originate within the rhetorical triangle—ethos, pathos, and logos—but transcend those restrictive boundaries to give voice to countercultural narratives. For example, Black rhetoric in the liberation tradition enacts the performance of communal identities embodied by Black experiences and empowered by biblical narratives.[9] Black protest narratives inspire other writers, scholars, and performers to action. Black rhetoricians empower readers to acquire a different understanding of Black people and the ethnographic evolution of Black culture.[10] This communal identity welcomes the engagement of new audiences, invokes a visible call for justice, and invites other voices to respond.[11] Black rhetoric constructs evocative narratives[12] to compel other communities to bear witness to its significance. Similarly, studying Black rhetoric interrogates the specific alienation between Black people, White people, and other people of color.[13] It also conveys the need for clear understanding, invites dialectic symmetry, and evokes dialogue intended to eliminate existing disconnects. The study of Black rhetoric engages spectators to bear witness, recognizes the inalienable rights of man, and amplifies the voices of people who survived centuries of censorship and silencing. Therefore, excavation of womanist theology must begin within the epistemological framework of Black rhetoric.

AN INVITATIONAL RHETORIC

As an expansion of the rhetoric from the Black Arts Movement of the 1960s and feminist rhetorical theories of the late twentieth century, womanist theology also assumes a communal identity, influenced by common experiences.[14] Womanist theology reflects an evocative biblical narrative and compels the women of today to reconnect and bear witness to the significance of sisterhood in the past, present, and future.[15] Unlike traditional White Anglo-Saxon Protestant patriarchal narratives, womanist theology advances invitational rhetoric to invoke identification and inclusion, in lieu of separation and exclusion.[16]

Womanist theology builds bridges between diverse communities and establishes external conditions to create a safe space for divergent perspectives to coexist and collectively construct catharsis as the foundation for a beloved community to flourish.[17] Womanist theological pedagogy concerns itself with the intertextuality of race, class, gender, and theology, without ignoring the existence of other voices and the validity of those perspectives. This inquiry illuminates the dialectic tension: extracted from feminist rhetorical theory, enacted through performative writing[18] and evocative narratives, embodied through performance ethnography,[19] and ultimately empowered through the terministic critical lens[20] of womanist theology, grounded in invitational rhetoric.

This exploration focuses on identifying invitational rhetoric; however, it does not ignore the existence of other voices and the validity of divergent perspectives. One way for women of color to build God's beloved community without boundaries and barriers is to collectively harness invitational rhetoric to tap into the healing potential of womanist theology for women from all faith traditions. This challenges the tenets of conquest-driven "religious rhetoric," regardless of historical, cultural, and contextual connections; creates safe spaces to convene convergent conversations and transform the way we think about sisterhood and ourselves;[21] and constructs sisterhood connections beyond the boundaries of "religious" books and belief systems. This critical ethnographic analysis examines the universal elements of biblical sisterhood and seeks to showcase how womanist theology weaves together the power of performance and evocative narratives in any context and, thus, opens the door to build bridges between traditionally marginalized and divergent communities. Building the beloved community does not require every brick look exactly alike; it merely requires they fit together to serve a common purpose. At the same time, it seeks to dispel the traditional theological dynamics of white male hegemony, paternal power, and privilege and invites womanist rhetorical pedagogy and praxis to build the beloved community for past, present, and future generations of sisterhood in all four corners of the globe.

MARRYING RHETORIC AND PERFORMANCE

Womanist theology invokes the call for creation within copresent communities, which coexist as countercultures within society.[22] In this way, it gives birth to both femininity and Blackness and harmonizes rhetoric and performance. Black rhetoric and performance breathe life into Black experiences. More often than not, rhetoric emerges as a free-will offering, making it an elective choice. Performance, on the other hand, sometimes occurs as a consequence, absent assent or choice.

Additionally, people often develop their perspective on another person's identity based upon what they see. This aspect of performance exists outside the control of the performer because performance conveys purpose through perspective. However, perspective does not dictate identity. Therefore, building the rhetorical foundation for the beloved community begins with an inquiry into the intersections of identity, community, and performativity.[23]

Rhetoric and performance coexist on interconnected planes, which means they mutually influence one another.[24] Rhetoric provides a linguistic tool to redefine and realign performance. Conversely, performance gives rhetoric a multidimensional perspective. Why does this matter? The intertextuality of rhetoric and performance produces personal testimony.

Testimony serves as more than a simple literary device. Testimony gives voice to different perspectives, creates space for mitigating any trauma triggered by the disconnect between rhetoric and performance, and opens the door for mutual understanding. Why is this important? Testimony invites changes in perspective, without necessitating any changes in performance. Thus, as a rhetoric tool, testimony is indispensable, because it allows room for more than one privileged perspective. This means the "testimonial encounter" possesses the potential power to simultaneously bring healing to the performer and audience, even if their perspectives differ.[25]

Why is the performance of Blackness and performative writing about the Black experience so necessary in this society? "Through enslavement, segregation, and discrimination, African Americans' culture has, in a sense, been 'colonized'; and appropriated."[26] African American women must continuously cultivate their own culture because "reasserting one's own cultural, social, and moral values and mores is, in part, the social process of decolonizing culture."[27] Performance covertly calls forth response and action, while rhetoric demands discussion.

I AM MY SISTERS' KEEPER: IMAGINE INVITATIONAL SISTERHOOD

Imagine a theological framework inspiring the sons and daughters of the Most High to protect, respect, and honor one another and exercise mutual understanding in lieu of envy. What if Cain recognized God created him in His Image, to serve as his brother's keeper,[28] just as certainly as He created Abel to keep watch over the sheep as their shepherd? What if Leah and Rachel learned to lovingly encircle, support, and pray for one another as sisters?[29] What if they joined together to pray for one another, pray for their children, and pray for Jacob, the husband both sisters loved? What if Leah and Rachel had argued less, prayed more, and praised the Most High with the fruit of their lips? "By him therefore let us offer the sacrifice of praise to God continually, that is, the fruit of our lips giving thanks to his name."[30]

Guided by invitational rhetoric, this interdisciplinary inquiry into womanist theology sought to create a safe space for sisterhood, critique the borders and boundaries of what sisterhood means, and call upon some biblical examples of what it means to keep or fail to keep our sisters. Psalms 121:5 exclaims: "The LORD is thy keeper: the LORD is thy shade upon thy right hand." *Does this mean we are not called to keep our sisters and hold one another accountable for supporting the circle of sisterhood?* Quite the contrary. If we reframe the question Cain asked in Genesis 4:9[31] and inquire of our Heavenly Father: *"Am I My Sisters' Keeper?"* we find Scripture replete with affirmative actions, showcasing sisterly support.

Through womanist theology, the Most High God compels us not to simply ask the rhetorical question but rather to enact, empower, and embody the answer, not merely through words but, more importantly, through our thoughts and actions. Ask yourself, "Am I my sisters' keeper?" Then, take some time to self-reflect to make sure your actions align with your answer. If we learned anything from our foremothers, Leah and Rachel, and the stories of our other sisters scattered throughout the Bible, we must remember the power to perform our purpose progresses as we pursue God through prayer and praise. For this reason, sisters must *keep* one another by continually calling out their names before the Most High God in prayer. Why? Because keeping my sisters in prayer strengthens my entire circle of sisterhood.

Sister keepers practice the principle that prayer as well as praise provides the perfect prescription to dispel disparity and empower prosperity. This means no matter what happens between my sisters and me, I will always *keep* my sisters in prayer. Prayer and praise represent the same literal, physical, and spiritual alignment of rhetoric and performance enacted in creation. When a woman practices prayer and praise, not only for herself and her family but also for her sisters, she performs her God-ordained purpose, plants the seeds of sisterhood, and propagates "fruitful"[32] interpersonal relationships to "Let brotherly (and sisterly) love continue."[33]

WOMEN WHO PRAY[34]

Women who pray must be strong
forbearing to remove mountains that do not belong
gaining power through prayer to conquer evil and wrong
humble faithful and virtuous praising Jesus in song.

Women who pray must read everyday
eating the word and careful what we do and say
letting Jesus fashion us like old dusty clay
unafraid and knowing when to say yea or nay.

Women who pray are meek
strengthened by the Lord of Hosts when we are weak
waiting for deliverance and answers to prayers we seek
steadfast and of good courage not at all oblique.

Women who pray are full of joy
careful not to let Satan sneak in and destroy

delightful in our daily due and employ
rejoicing in faith when others aim to annoy.

Women who pray are bold
not letting hurt and pain turn us bitter and cold
striving to be part of God's saintly fold
forgiving and charitable no goodness do we withhold.

Women who pray are cunningly wise
letting their ear receive word from God's eyes
wailing for the nation as we rise
teaching our daughters to moan lamenting cries.

NOTES

1. Tracey C. Bass, *The Poetic Scholar* (Ypsilanti, MI: I AM Media Books, 2020).

2. Genesis 1:3.

3. G.J. Shepherd, J. St. John, and T. Striphas, eds., *Communication As . . . Perspectives on Theory* (Thousand Oaks, CA: Sage, 2006)

4. Kreuter and Skinner (2000) define tailoring as, "Any combination of information or change strategies *intended to reach one specific person*, based on characteristics that are unique to that person, related to the outcome of interest, and have been *derived from an individual assessment*" (p. 1).

5. "In her essay 'Performance Practice as a Sire of Opposition,' cultural critic and feminist scholar, bell hooks, suggests that there are two modes of black performance—one ritualistic as a part of culture building and one manipulative out of necessity for survival in an oppressive world (1995, p. 210). Hooks suggests that these two are not mutually exclusive but bound together in dialogic tension given the way the skills endemic to black expressive culture are both required and deployed for ritual play and restrictive action." E. Patrick Johnson, "Black Performance Studies. Genealogies, Politics, Futures," in *The SAGE Handbook of Performance Studies*, ed. D. Soiyini Madison (Thousand Oaks, CA: Sage Publications, 2006) (p. 452).

6. The rhetorical tradition dates back to ancient times. Corax and Tisias first formally articulated rhetoric as an art (Aristotle, 1959, p. xii–xiii). Aristotle, considered the father of modern rhetoric, classifies rhetoric as "a counterpart of dialectic" and situates the rhetorical in direct contrast with the "strictly scientific" (p. xxxv).

7. Ibid.

8. Kenneth Burke. *A Rhetoric of Motives*. Vol. 178 (University of California Press, 1969).

9. E Patrick Johnson contends: "'Black' and 'performance': These two tropes complement one another in a dialectic that becomes an ontology of racialized cultural production. 'Blackness,' for instance, is a simulacrum until it is practiced—i.e., performed. The epistemological moment of race manifests itself in and through

performance in that performance facilitates self-and cultural reflexivity—a knowing made manifest by a 'doing.' Far from undergirding an essentialist purview of blackness, performance, as a mode of representation, emphasizes that, 'it is only through the way in which we come to know how we are constituted and who we are' (Hall, 1992, p. 30)" (p. 446). He further assuages: "While black performance has been sustaining and galvanizing force of black culture and a contributor to world culture at large, it has not always been recognized as a site of theorization in the academy. Similarly marginalized as the black bodies with which it is associated, black performance, while always already embedded within institutionally sanctioned and privileged forms of performance, has often been neglected as an intellectual site of inquiry" (p. 447). For these and many other reasons, womanist theology serves as a critical intellectual site of inquiry for scholars interested in its intersections.

10. Gergen and Gergen (2002) present ethnographic research as relationship formation, noting the relationship between rhetor and reader, researcher and audience. They contend that "there is one relational domain that has received little attention to date, that is, the relationship between rhetor and readerm researcher and audience." Additionally, the authors assert: "Our words constitute forms of action that invite others into certain forms of relationship as opposed to others. Thus our manner of writing and speaking contributes to life forms that may be extended throughout the educational sphere and into public modes of existence" (p. 13). In this way, Black rhetoric, performance, and performative writing engage Black and non-Black audiences who might otherwise not relate to the rhetor outside of the context of audiencing their research.

11. Christian preacher Kenneth Waters investigates "blackness" within the biblical context. His scholarly exploration of Afrocentricity gives voice to suppositions that shake the very core of Christianity. Waters positions Africa and people of African descent within the fulcrum of inquiry, surmising Afrocentricity "is solidly supported by evidence from various fields of investigation including archeology and paleontology, linguistics, anthropology, iconography, and historiography" (p. 1).

12. Arthur P. Bochner and Carolyn Ellis. "The ICQI and the Rise of Autoethnography: Solidarity through Community." *International Review of Qualitative Research* 9, no. 2 (August 2016): 208–217. doi:10.1525/irqr.2016.9.2.208.

13. The performance of blackness brings rhetoric and performance into alignment as the Black experience brings to bear rhetorical responses to racism in everyday actions. "Because no performance exists outside the politics of representation, ideology is embedded within them and thus thrusts black performance into the center of identity politics as performers struggle over the most effective or 'proper' performances to deploy against racism" (p. 457). For this reason, E Patrick Johnson sees Black rhetoric as a stop gap: "Black performance as a mode of resistance functions to suture the gap between the oppressor and the oppressed, the vocal and voiceless, the dominator and the dominated" (p. 457).

14. H Hathaway. Rewriting Race, Gender and Religion in Toni Morrison's Song of Solomon and Paradise. *Religions* 10 (2019), 345.

15. Renita Weems, *Just a Sister Away: Understanding the Timeless Connection between Women of Today and Women in the Bible* (New York, NY: Warner Books, 2005).

16. Sonja K. Foss and Cindy L. Griffin. "Beyond Persuasion: A Proposal for an Invitational Rhetoric." *Communications Monographs* 62, no. 1 (1995): 2–18.

17. Roxanne R. Reed. "The Restorative Power of Sound: A Case for Communal Catharsis in Toni Morrison's 'Beloved'." *Journal of Feminist Studies in Religion* 23, no. 1 (2007): 55–71. Accessed June 4, 2020. www.jstor.org/stable/20487887.

18. In *"Skin Flint (or, the Garbage Man's Kid):* A Generative Autobiographical Performance Based on Tami Spry's *Tattoo Stories,"* performance studies scholar Bryant Keith Alexander explains, "Performance methodology engages both performer and audience in a sensuous activity of embodied experience" (p. 99). Alexander further contends: "Victor Turner defines 'performative reflexivity,' as 'a condition in which a socio-cultural group, or its most perceptive members acting representatively turn, bend back or reflect upon themselves'" (24). "While Turner's thoughts on reflexivity is culture and context specific, in generative autobiography I am interested in this critical reflection as it can be applied to the role of the audience member of autobiographical performance. The inherent reflexive turn of performative experience is precisely its power to transmit, as well as critique culture. The reflexive turn becomes a critical move of making sense of lived experience triggered by a performance of bending the critical eye inward" (pp. 100–101). *Text and Performance Quarterly* 20. 1 (2000): 97–14.

19. Dwight Conquergood. *Cultural Struggles: Performance, Ethnography, Praxis* (University of Michigan Press, 2013).

20. Kenneth Burke. *Language as Symbolic Action: Essays on Life, Literature, and Method* (University of California Press, 1966).

21. Kathryn D. Cramer and Hank Wasiak, *Change the Way You See Yourself: through Asset-Based Thinking* (Philadelphia; London: Running Press, 2008).

22. Genesis 1 provides an introduction to the Creator, the Most High God of all creation, who "created the heaven and the earth" in Genesis 1:1; "created great whales, and every living creature that moveth" in Genesis 1:21; and created the capstone of creation in Genesis 1:27, when He "created man in his own image, in the image of God created he him; male and female created he them" (KJV). Thus, God created "female" in His own image, presented her to Adam, whom He also created in His image, as "an help meet for him." Adam received her, and he declared: "This is now bone of my bones, and flesh of my flesh: she shall be called Woman, because she was taken out of Man." Genesis 1 and 2 demonstrate the rhetorical and performative power of creation, as well as woman's call to cocreate and coexist with man, making the pedagogy of womanist theology a natural progression toward the fulfillment of woman's purpose "in the beginning."

23. Womanist theology focuses on the simultaneous performance of "femininity" and "blackness" and the convergence of these dual identities as countercultures within the dominant culture of white patriarchal society. This necessitates the interrogation of identity, community, and performativity to isolate the silenced voice of black women throughout history. In "The Cult of True Womanhood: Toward a

Womanist Attitude in African-American Theatre," feminist rhetoric scholar Gloria Dickerson asserts: "That voice has been silenced for centuries, breaking forth sporadically, choked, and gasping for air. It has been silenced by the obvious foot on the throat and the subtle whispering thought. It has been silenced as part and parcel of the corruption of the ancient matriarchy. The depiction and perception of African American woman in this country through stereotypes has garbled her voice and distorted her image. The real tragedy is that the African American woman herself has too frequently bought that distortion" (p. 110). In this way, white patriarchal society not only silences the voice of the woman of color but also systematically seeks to erase her image. Dickerson further contends: "The image of the African-American woman has been sullied on the world stage. The trick for her now is reclaim that image through self-definition, using Nommo, the magic power of the word; uncategorically rejecting the stereotypes which are not 'my shame' (as Harriet Tubman said), they are the shame of the perpetrators" (p. 111). Dickerson concludes: "Not only is the language of oppression the same the world over; the anguish of women is echoed around the world and resonates from continent to continent" (p. 112). In other words, silence, isolation, and erasure extend beyond the boundaries of the language, culture, and geography of African American women, invoking a global silencing of women of color across the African diaspora.

24. Womanist theology creates a safe space to integrate race, gender, and theology, without sacrificing one over the other. It also gives voice to the complex personal testimonies, encompassing the identities, communities, and performativity of women of color. In *Behind the Mask of the Strong Black Woman: Voice and the Embodiment of a Costly Performance*, feminist performance scholar Tamara Beauboeuf-Lafontant argues: "Voice-centered (rather than discourse-focused) research highlights the complexity of subjectivity. Attending to the overlooked and distorted experiences of women, voice-centered inquiry has sought to access and understand a central dynamic: the distinctions between cultural understandings of women of how they are *supposed* to think, feel, and act, and the perspectives or voices of individual women that are relatively free from second thoughts and instant revision" (p. 9). Moreover, she warns other scholars, the tendency of the dominant social class "to focus on women's voices rather than prevailing social discourses is a subversive act of 'creat[ing] the space for an absent subject. It is also an intentional attempt to access the 'subjugated knowledge' that oppressed groups and individuals create in order to sustain themselves in situations of inequity" (p. 9). Tamara Beauboeuf-Lafontant. *Behind the Mask of the Strong Black Woman. Voice and the Embodiment of a Costly Performance* (Philadelphia, PA: Temple University Press, 2009).

25. Womanist theology represents the embodiment of testimony; the scholarship interrogates the intracultural and intercultural interactions between women of color and the dominant "other," whether white male, white female, black male, or any other contrary perspective. In this way, womanist theology unites diverse perspectives through testimony. Scholar Jennifer Griffith acknowledges, "Testimony, therefore, exposes the vulnerability of listeners as well. They must face their limitations, their mortality, through the story of another's trauma" (p. 2). Griffiths surmises, "Testimony offers a public enactment of memory, and clearly, the cultural context

and content work collaboratively to shape testimony. When looking at the reception of testimony within specific contexts, one must also consider cultural inscriptions of identity" (p. 4). Jennifer Griffiths. *Traumatic Possessions. The Body and Memory in African American Women's Writing and Performance* (Charlottesville: University of Virginia Press, 2009)

26. Deseriee Kennedy. "Decolonizing Culture: The Media, Black Women, and Law." In *Stepping Forward. Black Women in Africa and the Americas*, eds. Catherine Higgs, Barbara A. Moss, and Earline Rae Ferguson (Athens, OH: Ohio University Press, 2002), 257.

27. Ibid.

28. The Most High God created Adam in His image and assigned Adam to guard and protect the garden. Genesis 2:15 says: "And the LORD God took the man, and put him into the garden of Eden to dress it and to keep it." The Hebrew word for keep, Strong's keyword number is H8104, rendered as רמָשׁ in Hebrew, is shâmar, pronounced shaw-mar', which means " properly to hedge about (as with thorns), that is, guard; generally to protect, attend to, etc.: beware, be circumspect, take heed (to self), keep (-er, self), mark, look narrowly, observe, preserve, regard, reserve, save (self), sure, (that lay) wait (for), watch (-man)." The assignment God gave to Adam in the garden applies to every seed and living thing past, present, and future. God never revoked Adam's assignment after Adam and Eve transgressed; rather, God cursed the ground (Genesis 3:17–19). God also cursed woman's most interpersonal relation-ships, with her children and her husband (Genesis 3:16). Adam's response literally breathed new life into their relationship and assigned the woman a new purpose: "And Adam called his wife's name Eve; because she was the mother of all living" (Genesis 3:20). Adam and Eve's assignments to keep and give birth to living seeds evolved to evoke our purpose and performance today.

29. Esword notes the Strong's concordance keyword for sister H269, rendered as תוֹחָא in Hebrew, is *'âchôth*, pronounced as aw-khoth'. The four Hebrew letters that make up the Hebrew word 'âchôth provide insight into the purpose and performance of sisterhood. The first Hebrew letter, Aleph, represented by the pictorial image of an ox head, means "Strong, Power, Leader." The second Hebrew letter, Chet, repre-sented by the pictorial image of a tent wall, means "Outside, Divide, Half." The third Hebrew letter, Vav, represented by the pictorial image of a tent peg, means "Add, Secure, Hook." The fourth Hebrew letter, Tav, represented by the pictorial image of crossed sticks, means "Mark, Sign, Signal, Monument." Taken together, the Hebrew letters in the word "sister" mean sisters were created to serve as strong leaders who stand outside the divide to add security and stability and provide a mark, sign, or signal. The visual image of sisterhood is a never-ending circle, where sisters mutu-ally support one another. Each sister supports the sister in front of her while being supported by the sister behind her. In this way the circle of sisterhood depends on each sister searching for the sister who needs her support and stepping up to lend her support, rather than seeking support. This makes sisterhood an act of humble service.

30. Hebrews 3:15.

31. Genesis 4:9: "And the LORD said unto Cain, Where is Abel thy brother? And he said, I know not: Am I my brother's keeper?"

32. Fruitful interpersonal relationships follow the Most High God's commandment on the sixth day of creation in Genesis 1:28: "And God blessed them, and God said unto them, Be fruitful, and multiply, and replenish the earth, and subdue it: and have dominion over the fish of the sea, and over the fowl of the air, and over every living thing that moveth upon the earth." Furthermore, fruitful relationships are fueled by the Spirit of the Most High, as outlined in Galatians 5:22–23: "But the fruit of the Spirit is love, joy, peace, longsuffering, gentleness, goodness, faith, meekness, temperance: against such there is no law."

33. Hebrews 13:1.

34. "Women Who Pray" by Michelle Rhnea Yisrael, excerpt from *The Enemy Within* (Ypsilanti, MI: I AM Media Books, 2019).

BIBLIOGRAPHY

Alexander, Bryant Keith. 2000. "Skin Flint (or, the Garbage Man's Kid): A Generative Autobiographical Performace Based on Tami Spry's Tattoo Stories." *Text and Performace Quarterly* 97–114.

Aristotle. 1959. *The "Art" of Rhetoric.* Translated by J.H. Freese. Vol. 22. Cambridge, MA: Harvard University Press.

Beauboeuf-Lafontant, Tamara. 2009. *Behind the Mask of the Strong Black Woman: Voice and the Embodiment of a Costly Performance.* Philadelphia, PA: Temple University Press.

Bochner, Arthur P., and Carolyn Ellis. 2016. *Evocative Autoethnography: Writing Lives and Telling Stories.* Walnut Creek, CA: Left Coast Press.

Bochner, Arthur P., and Carolyn Ellis. 2016. "The ICQI and the Rise of Autoethnography: Solidarity." *International Review of Qualitative Research* 9 (2): 208–217. doi:10.1525/irqr.2016.9.2.208.

Burke, Kenneth. 1969. *A Rhetoric of Motives.* Vol. 178. University of California Press.

———. 1966. *Language As Symbolic Action: Essays on Life, Literature, and Method.* University of California Press.

Conquergood, Dwight. 2013. *Cultural Struggles: Performance, Ethnography, Praxis.* Ann Arbor, MI: University of Michigan Press.

Cramer, Kathryn D., and Hank Wasiak. 2008. *Change the Way You See Yourself: Through Asset-Based Thinking.* Philadelphia, PA: Running Press.

Dickerson, Glenda. 1988. "The Cult of True Womanhood: Toward a Womanist Attitude in African-American Theatre." *Theatre Journal* 40 (2): 178–187.

Foss, Sonja K., and Griffin L. Cindy. 1995. "Beyond Persuasion: A Proposal for an Invitational Rhetoric." *Communication Monographs* 62 (1): 2–18.

Gergen, Mary M., and Kenneth J. Gergen. 2002. "Ethnograpic Representation as Relationship." In *Ethnographically Speaking: Autoethnography, Literature, and Aesthetics*, edited by Arthur P. Bochner and Carolyn Eliis. Walnut Creek, CA: AltaMira Press.

Griffiths, Jennifer. 2009. *Traumatic Possessions: The Body and Memory in African American Women's Writing and Performance.* Charlottsville, VA: University of Virginia Press.

Hathaway, H. 2019. "Rewriting Race, Gender and Religion in Toni Morrison's Song of Solomon and Paradise." *Religions* 10 (6): 345–356.

Johnson, E. Patrick. 2006. "Black Performance Studies: Genealogies, Politics, Futures." In *The SAGE Handbook of Performance Studies*, edited by D. Soiyini Madison. Thousand Oaks, CA: Sage Publications.

Kennedy, Deseriee. 2002. "Decolonizing Culture: The Media, Black Women and Law." In *Stepping Forward: Black Women in Africa and the Americas*, edited by Catherine Higgs, Barbara A. Moss and Earline Rae Ferguson, 257–270. Athens, OH: Ohio University Press.

Kreuter, M. W., and C. S. Skinner. 2000. "Tailoring: What's in a Name?" *Health Education Research* 15 (1): 1–4.

Reed, Roxanne R. 2007. "The Restorative Power of Sound: A Case for Communal Catharsis in Toni Morrison's 'Beloved'." *Journal of Feminist Studies in Religion* 23 (1): 55–71.

Shepherd, G. J., J. St. John, and T. Striphas, . 2006. *Commuication as . . . Perspectives on Theory.* Thousand Oaks, CA: Sage Publications.

Waters, Kenneth L. 1993. *Afrocentric Sermons: The Beauty of Blackness in the Bible.* Valley Forge, PA: Judson Press.

Weems, Renita. 2005. *Just a Sister Away: Understanding the Timeless Connection between Women of Today and Women in the Bible.* New York, NY: Warner Books.

Yisrael, Michelle Rhnea. 2019. *The Enemy Within.* Ypsilanti, MI: I AM Media Books.

Conclusion

Annette D. Madlock and Cerise L. Glenn

As we write the brief closing remarks to this edited collection, we are living through simultaneous seminal historical events. Presumptive presidential democratic nominee Joe Biden has chosen Senator Kamala Harris (CA) as his running mate for vice president. She is the first woman of color on a major party ticket. Johns Hopkins reported[1] that the United States has gone from 4 million to over 8 million cases of COVID-19 in just over 30 days, and the Black Lives Matter movement has taken on global significance. We are living in turbulent times. As Chanequa Walker-Barnes states:

> For many of us, the propulsion toward justice is the fire shut up in our bones. It consumes us and will not let up. We remain hypervigilant for the signs and costs of racial oppression. When we work from an intersectional framework, our alertness is multiply magnified. Our social media feeds are filled with news and commentary about the latest high-profile incident of systemic oppression. Indeed our close connections with other racial justice workers often mean that we learn about these incidents before they gain national media attention. We are ready to engage and to act when these incidents arise.[2]

Like many other professionals in this line of work, Annette and Cerise, co-editors, believe and have stated that Black scholarship is not an undertaking just for the sake of scholarship, research and analysis for the sake of research and analysis, and publication for the sole purpose of publication. The work begins and ends within the communities that each one of us finds ourselves engaged. The contributors to this collection have a fire shut up in their bones and are working to fight against systemic oppression beyond the words found on these pages.

NOTES

1. All COVID-19 information presented here is from the https://coronavirus.jhu
.edu/map.html. Reported 8/13/20, 5:27:25 p.m. Global cases 20,739,537, global
deaths 751,910. U.S. cases 5,242,184, U.S. deaths 166,971.

2. Chanequa Walker Barnes. I bring the voices of my people—a womanist vision
for racial reconciliation. Michigan, William B. Earmans Publishing Company (2019,
p. 221).

BIBLIOGRAPHY

https://gisanddata.maps.arcgis.com/apps/opsdashboard/index.html#/bda7594740f
d40299423467b48e9ecf6

Index

abuse, 36–39, 43–44, 55, 67
African American, xiii–xviii, 3, 9, 17, 19–20, 33–36, 39–42, 44, 51–52, 54–56, 60, 74, 77–79, 82–83, 94
Africana Womanism, 2
Afrocentric, 54–55
Afrocentric pedagogy, 54
Alexander, Michelle, 31
antioppressionist, 3, 9, 57–58

beloved community, xvii, 51–53, 58–59, 63, 65, 67, 69–74, 92–93
bias, 26, 39
Biden, Joe, xvii, 103
bilingualism, 53
black feminism, xiii, 34
black feminist thought, xvii, 33–35, 42, 45
Black Lives Matter, xvi–xvii, 2, 8–9, 17–21, 23, 25, 28, 39–42, 103
Blackmon, Traci, 21–22
black press, 4, 11–12. *See also Milwaukee Community Journal*; *Milwaukee Courier*
black womanhood, xv, xvii, 34, 63–64, 66, 68–69, 71–73
Brown, Hallie Quinn, 77, 81, 85
Brown, Michael, 18, 21–22, 40

Cannon, Katie Geneva, xiii–xviii, 3, 9
Cardi B., 66
church, xiii–xv, xvii, 3, 7–9, 19, 21–22, 33–45, 58, 77–85; African Methodist Episcopal, 21, 77, 81, 85; AME, 21, 77–79, 81–85; Baptist, 8, 38, 81, 84; black church, xiv, xvii, 21, 34–38, 40–45, 80; United Church of Christ (UCC), 21
Collins, Patricia Hill, 34
communitarian, 57
conservative, xvii, 1–3, 5, 7, 35, 38
Cooper, Brittney, 21, 74
COVID-19, 1, 103–104
culturally mismatched, 51, 55

daughter, 9, 33, 36–37, 78–79, 94
domestic violence, 35

education, xv–xvi, 3, 8–9, 25–26, 51, 53–54, 56–60, 71, 82–83
equality, 2–3, 7, 25, 27, 53, 78, 82–83, 85
equity, 7–8, 28, 85
Evangelical, 1–3, 5–8

feminism, xiii, xvi, 34
Floyd, George, xvi, 1, 40

Francis, Leah Gunning, 21, 29

Garza, Alicia, 18, 29

Harris, Kamala, 103
historiography, 77
Hudson-Weems, Clenora, 2

intragroup dynamics, 39, 41–42
invisibility, 20, 68
invitational rhetoric, 91–95

Jones, Melanie C., 35
Julia, Cooper, Anna, 54, 57

King, Martin Luther, Jr., 20, 22–23, 28, 63, 70, 83

law enforcement, 18, 40
leader, 19, 43, 78. *See also* Murphy McKenzie, Vashti; Wells Barnett, Ida B.
leaders, xvi, 4, 20–21, 37–38, 41, 45, 78, 81, 83. *See also* Murphy McKenzie, Vashti
leadership, xvi–xvii, 19–21, 29, 33, 35, 37–38, 41–42, 77–80, 83–85. *See also* Murphy McKenzie, Vashti; Wells Barnett, Ida B.
Lederer, Laura, 2
Lee, Jarena, 77–78, 85. *See also* African Methodist Episcopal; black church; womanist theologian; women in leadership
LGBTQIAP, 2; LGBTQIA, 29; queer, 2, 18, 21, 38, 74
liberation theology, 59
liberatory bilingualism, 53
Lightsey, Pamela, 21. *See also* womanist theologian
Lizzo, 64–66, 73–74

Martin, Trayvon, 17–18, 29, 40
Milwaukee Community Journal, 4. *See also* black press; newspaper

Milwaukee Courier, 4. *See also* black press; newspaper
Milwaukee Journal, 4
mother, xv–xvi, 2, 5, 9, 33–34, 36–39, 45, 63, 73–74
motherhood, 57, 59, 68
multicultural education, 51, 56, 60
Murphy McKenzie, Vashti, 85. *See also* leader; leaders; leadership

National Basketball Association, xvii
nationalism, 7, 17, 22, 24–25, 28; American nationalism, 17, 22, 24; Black nationalist, 21; Christian nationalism, 7
newspaper, 5, 87–88. *See also* black press; *Milwaukee Community Journal*; *Milwaukee Courier*

Obama, Barack, 8, 68
Obama, Michelle, 66, 68
Ogunyemi, Chikwenye Okonojo, 2
Ore, Ersula J., 17, 29

police, xvi, 17–18, 21–22, 35, 38–43, 64–65; police brutality, 21, 39–40; policing, 33, 40, 66, 68

Rachet womanism, 64–66; ratchetness, 66–67, 69–70, 74
racism, xiv–xv, 2, 5, 8, 18, 34, 36, 40, 44, 58–59, 65, 68, 70
relationships, 36, 43–45, 73, 95
representation, 21, 56, 66, 85
respectability politics, xiv, 20–21, 28, 35, 37–38, 43, 66–67, 71–73. *See also* Wells Barnett, Ida B.
respectable, 35, 38, 63

sacred space, 59. *See also* spirituality
Satchel, Rosalyn, 21
sermon, 24, 38–39, 79
social justice, xiv, xvi–xvii, 1–2, 4, 7–8, 19, 21, 29, 33, 37, 40–43, 45, 51–53, 57–58

Social Justice Institute, 21
social media, xvi, 4, 8–9, 22
social movements, 18, 42, 52
spirituality, 33–34, 36–37, 41–45, 57, 59
student nonviolent coordinating
    committee, 19

Taylor, Breonna, xvi–xvii, 40
theology, xiii–xv, 3, 8–9, 59, 74, 78–79,
    85, 91–95
theopolitical, 3, 7
theory, 2–3, 34, 53, 55, 57, 92
Thurman, Howard, 59
Tometi, Opal, 18
transgender, 2. *See also* LGBTQIA;
    LGBTQIAP; queer
Trump, Donald J., 5, 23, 27

vernacular, 9, 57–58. *See also* culturally
    mismatched; liberatory bilingualism;
    multicultural education

Walker, Alice, 2, 22, 34, 45
Wells Barnett, Ida B., 9. *See also* leader;
    leadership; respectability politics;
    womanist

white supremacist, 71, 74
wife, 9, 38, 43, 78
Williams, Jamye Coleman, 77, 83, 85
womanish, 34
womanism, xiii–xviii, 2–3, 9, 22,
    28–29, 33–34, 39–40, 42, 51, 57,
    63–74
womanist, xiii–xiv, xvi–xvii, 1–5, 7, 9,
    17, 19–23, 25, 27–29, 35, 37, 42,
    45, 51–60, 65–70, 73–74, 77–79, 85,
    91–95, 104. *See also* Wells Barnett,
    Ida B.
womanist pedagogy, 52–57, 59–60. *See
    also* afrocentric pedagogy; culturally
    mismatched
womanist theologian, 21
women in leadership, 35, 78. *See also*
    Brown, Hallie Quinn; Cannon,
    Katie Geneva; Garza, Alicia; Harris,
    Kamala; Julia, Cooper, Anna; Lee,
    Jarena
Women's National Basketball
    Association, xvii

Zimmerman, George, 17–18. *See also*
    law enforcement; police

About the Editors

Annette D. Madlock completed her doctoral work at Howard University with distinction. She is an ordained minister and chaplain, independent scholar, community and women's health advocate, and technical communicator with a passion for writing and research, along with a knack for simplifying complex information for diverse audiences. Dr. Madlock is an award-winning author with more than forty publications and over fifty national and international professional presentations and workshops. Dr. Madlock's notable books include *Health Communication and Breast Cancer among Black Women: Culture, Identity, Spirituality, and Strength* (Lexington Books) and *Communicating Women's Health: Social and Cultural Norms that Influence Health Decisions* (Routledge). Her forthcoming work includes *the Journal of Communication and Religion Special Issue: "A Womanist Rhetorical Vision for Building the Beloved Community,"* where she serves as a guest editor, and *The Power of "RE": An Inspirational Guide on How to REdo, REvise, and REsubmit for Those Second Chances in Life* (Creative Legacy Books) *and Kwanzaa Curriculum for the 21st Century* (Creative Legacy Books).

Dr. Madlock was named one of the Eastern Communication Association's Distinguished Teaching Fellows. In her spare time, she shares her love for writing at www.sistercirclewriters.com and her advocacy work at www .thepinkandtheblack.com. Dr. Annette also loves to travel and spend time with family and friends. If you want to know more about Dr. Annette D. Madlock, follow her on social media: Twitter @AMadlock, @SisterWriters, @PNKBLKPRJ; Facebook and Instagram @The Pink and The Black Project, @Sister Circle Writers.

Cerise L. Glenn (PhD, Howard University) is an associate professor in the department of Communication Studies at the University of North Carolina at Greensboro. She has also served as the director of the African American and African Diaspora Studies program. One of her research interests centers on the professional and social identity of underrepresented groups, and she mentors diverse groups in higher education from intersectional perspectives. She also examines how African American women negotiate their identities utilizing Black feminist and womanist thought. Currently, she is the principal investigator on a $1 million multiyear National Science Foundation ADVANCE grant, which strengthens organizational practices to recruit and retain women faculty in the STEM fields. Honors include receiving The Order of Pisgah Award for Alumni Achievement, from the University of North Carolina at Asheville in 2020. She was awarded the 2016 Outstanding Book Chapter of the Year, African American Communication and Culture Division of the National Communication Association, for her chapter on mentoring experiences of African American female graduate students. She was also awarded the Feminist Teacher-Mentor Award, Organization for the Study of Communication Language and Gender in 2016.

About the Contributors

Kami Anderson, PhD, is an interculturalist, scholar, and language advocate. Originally from Milwaukee, Wisconsin, Dr. Anderson has always kept a tight grip on her passion and compassion for others and difference through language. Her primary focus is family empowerment through language with an emphasis on application and confidence. She holds a bachelor's degree in Spanish from Spelman College, a master's degree in international affairs/interdisciplinary studies in international communication and anthropology from American University, and a PhD in communication and culture from Howard University.

Dr. Kami Anderson has published extensively in both English and Spanish in scholarly and trade journals as well as in national U.S. news publications. In addition to *From Sabotage to Support: A New Vision for Feminist Solidarity in the Workplace*, coauthored with Dr. Joy Wiggins, she has published several other books, including *Raising Bilingual Brown Babies: Everyday Strategies to Become a Confident Bilingual Family* (2018) and *Language, Identity and Choice: Raising Bilingual Children in a Global Society* (2015, Lexington Books), which talks about her own experiences raising her children bilingual.

Andre E. Johnson, PhD, is an associate professor of rhetoric and media studies in the Department of Communication and Film at the University of Memphis. He teaches classes in African American public address, rhetoric, race, religion, and interracial communication. Dr. Johnson is the author of *The Forgotten Prophet: Bishop Henry McNeal Turner and the African American Prophetic Tradition* (Lexington Books, 2012), the coauthor (with Amanda Nell Edgar, PhD) of *The Struggle over Black Lives Matter and All*

Lives Matter (Lexington Books, 2018), and the author of *No Future in This Country: The Prophetic Pessimism of Bishop Henry McNeal Turner* (2020).

Kimberly Johnson, PhD, is an associate professor of communications and women's studies at Tennessee State University in Nashville, Tennessee. She brings to the Department of Communications her areas of specialization: political, religious, and African American rhetoric, rhetorical criticism, cultural criticism, and womanism. Dr. Johnson teaches the senior project capstone course, communication research methods, honors public speaking, fundamentals of communication, public speaking, persuasion, African American rhetoric, and introduction to women's studies to undergraduate students. Dr. Johnson has presented her research at professional communication associations such as the National Communication Association, Rhetoric Society of America, Southern States Communication Association, and the Tennessee Communication Association. She is the author of *The Womanist Preacher: Proclaiming Womanist Rhetoric from the Pulpit* (Lexington Books, 2017). Her research interests lie at the intersection of rhetoric, race, and religion—more specifically, womanist rhetoric and womanist preaching, feminist rhetoric, African American sacred rhetoric, along with issues around power and social justice.

Dr. Johnson has a Doctor of Philosophy in communication along with a Graduate Certificate in women's and gender studies from the University of Memphis, a master of Divinity degree from McCormick Theological Seminary, and a bachelor of Science degree in speech from Northwestern University. She is a licensed and ordained minister in the Christian Church (Disciples of Christ). She serves as an associate minister at New Covenant Christian Church in Nashville, Tennessee, under the leadership of Rev. Dr. Judy D. Cummings.

Natonya Listach is a senior instructor and the assistant director of Forensics at Middle Tennessee State University. She is also a doctoral student in the department of Communication and Film at the University of Memphis. Her research focuses on race, gender, and religion with specific emphasis on African American rhetoric and public address. She is a member of the following organizations: National Communication Association, National Sorority of Phi Delta Kappa, Inc., Organization for the Study of Communication, Language and Gender, Southern States Communication Association, and Tennessee Communication Association. When she's not researching or teaching, she enjoys lazy days with her girls, Lizzy and Zayne, and her husband John.

Michelle Meggs, DAH, is a native of Brooklyn, New York. She earned her bachelor of Arts from Johnson C. Smith University, her Master of Divinity degree from Wake Forest University, and Doctor of Arts in humanities from Clark Atlanta University, with a focus on Africana women's studies. She currently serves as the executive director of the Women and Girls Research Alliance at UNC Charlotte. Her research and ministry interests are in the areas of black women's spirituality, black women's images in popular culture, and deconstructing the stereotypes that negatively impact black women's lives.

Tracy Coquette Bass is a doctoral student, poetic-scholar, researcher, and performance artist with over forty years of creative writing and production experience. She is a warrior for women's wellness, and her weapon is words. Known worldwide as the original Words Doctor, she founded I AM Media International to amplify silenced stories and give birth to the indigenous narratives of native people across the globe. She holds a master's degree in communication and a bachelor's in comprehensive communication and social science with Honors from Eastern Michigan University. Ahava also earned her master's in practical theology from Regent University. She graduated from the Geraldine Marvel Miller Wright Institute for Women in Ministry and is a licensed and ordained chaplain with the International Association of Chaplains in Roseville, Michigan. Studying early childhood education at Mott Community College in Flint, Michigan, ignited Ahava's passion for ministry and creativity. She went from Flint to full-blown FIYAH, when she left the memories of the Flint Water Crisis behind, relocated to Belize Central America, and founded The FIYAH Chaplain Association to serve the men, women, and children of Belize. Ahava is currently building her skills as a "media midwife" in Liberty University's doctoral program in strategic media.

Michelle Rhnea Yisrael has been honored to empower women and children for over thirty years. She has a master's degree in English from Chicago State University, a master's in online teaching from the University of Illinois Springfield, a soul degree in love, and possesses a passion for nurturing the human soul. Ms. Yisrael was a district leader for eight alternative high schools on the Southside of Chicago, where she trained and managed principals, teachers, and support staff. Additionally, she was the director of an alternative high school and dean of instruction for another. Ms. Yisrael has been an educational leader for thirty-seven years. She founded and operated an independent school for much of that time while managing a budget for two city-funded programs and two federally funded programs simultaneously. Currently, she is an assistant professor at Chicago's Kennedy-King College and is one of the education coaches for urbaneducoach.com. She is one of the coauthors of T.R.U.S.T. Classroom Management program. Professor Yisrael is a writer for I AM Media Books and author of *The Jeremiah 9 Woman: A 52-Week Prayer Journey*, *The Enemy Within: A Survivor's Story*, *In Each Moment: An Anthology of Short Stories about Life & Love*, and *Freedom to Engage: A Critical Auto-Ethnographic Analysis of a Community College Professor*.